Praise Fo

"Potter gives us a novel that echoes the soulful noir of Walter Mosley combined with the rising arc of a comic book. His protagonist—AJ, is driven by a relentless sense of justice as he discovers his true calling. He's a detective in the making, proving that sometimes the best person to find the truth is the one who's been watching from the sidelines all along."

Beta Reader: Randy Voss
Columbus, OH.

"In the gritty world of Baltimore, former Marine AJ discovers the hotel beverage department is just as dangerous as a combat zone. While his military precision and charm win over the staff, he must navigate a web of foes and an unscrupulous boss who wants him to fail. Armed with sharp observation skills and strong integrity, AJ soon finds himself uncovering corporate fraud and tracking down missing heirlooms. With the help of unlikely allies, potential lovers and his own life challenges, he discovers his calling."

Beta Reader: Jeremy Gordensky
New York City, NY.

The Accidental Detective #1

"Origin Story"

"Life is like a rat's maze,

And the deity that created it has gone

quite mad,

No longer remembering its purpose."

-Unknown Author-

Prologue

I heard him returning and tried my best to only take short breaths as I waited, looking up to the sidewalk from my hiding spot. When Egbert finally appeared, he strained to balance a computer monitor stacked on top of a dot matrix printer. He stopped at the side of the van, wrestling with the electronics, trying to slide the door open. As he continued his clumsiness, I tiptoed up the steps towards him.

Once I made it up to the sidewalk, I must have made a sound because Egbert suddenly looked over his shoulder in my direction. I rewarded this action by slapping his mask-covered head with the blackjack I was carrying. It whistled as I swung it, as if I was cranking a bat to hit a homerun. It landed along his jawline with a hard whap.

When it made contact, I was sure I had killed him, but then he softly said, "Oh, momma" as his knees collapsed beneath him and he started to slide down the side of the van. With one hand still on the sliding door, he tried to stop his fall by grabbing the handle, but it didn't help.

He was yanked sideways as the door slid open with a--*sshhhh*--dragging him along. When it came to a full stop with a loud *clunk,* the office equipment he was carrying flew from his arms.

The printer went to the left and made a loud scraping sound as it clattered to the sidewalk; pieces of plastic and metal bounced everywhere. The monitor flipped into the night air to the right. The screen exploded and showered the sidewalk with glass, breaking the silence of the night. I stood there watching as it continued to flip down the sidewalk like a scene from a movie in slow motion.

With the sudden noise, lights starting going on in a few apartments. A window above the bail bond office opened and a guy leaned out trying to get a view of what was happening on the other side of the van. He shouted "Egbert, you okay over there?"

His loud voice startled me but I reacted like I'd been taught: *Move fast, get in, and get out.* I squatted and rolled him Egbert. His chest was going up and down, so I was happy he was still alive, even though his jaw sat at a crooked angle. A long dribble of pink slobber ran out of his mouth beneath the mask, and a small trickle of blood seeped from his ear.

When I spied the gold chain at the nape of his neck, I reached down and snatched it, but it held firm. All I managed was to yank his head up, only for it to bang right back down on the red cobblestones. Ouch!

It took me a few seconds to locate the clasp on the necklace, and suddenly I smelled something like ammonia. I looked around for the source of the smell and saw a dark stain blooming from the front of Egbert's jeans, spreading up past his belt. He had pissed himself.

When I finally worked the clasp loose, I balled the necklace into my fist and shoved it into my pocket. A bundle of money stuck out the breast pocket of his flannel shirt, so I relieved him of that too.

A window above me suddenly opened and the old lady from earlier stuck her head out. She looked down at me standing over Egbert's prone body and then screamed for all she was worth. By the time she had gathered enough breath for another scream, I was already running.

Chapter 1

"It really doesn't make any sense carrying this thing around" I muffled under my breath.

As communication technology went, it was an antique. The battery barely held a charge and was so bulky that I've even frightened some guests because they thought I was carrying a gun under my suit jacket. Apart from those highlights, when I was the only manager left on duty, there was no one else here to contact me using so basically, I had to carry around a piece of equipment that served no purpose. I should just accept the fact that our discussion would end the same as before. He was not going to listen.

Whenever I had an idea or suggestion, he would point out in a not-so-subtle way that he was in charge. He'd pull rank and remind me that he had more experience and that I should just keep my mouth shut and do what he told me to do. Another person would probably keep quiet and go along with whatever he said to make their work-life easier, but that was not me. In situations where I knew I was right, acquiescing was a difficult pill to swallow.

Now, as I pleaded my case once again about the walkie-talkie, he wasn't listening. It's been a long time since I have been around a person I disliked this much and whenever I got within a few feet of him, I had to remind myself to keep calm, and not throttle him.

Since I started working here, we have had a strained relationship. At times, I swear I could see his antagonism floating around him like a green gas sometimes. I tried many times to figure out why he felt this way. Could it have been because he wasn't included in my interview process when I was hired? Or maybe it was the fact that although I had a background in management, I had no hospitality industry experience? I really didn't know and had given him as much benefit of the doubt that I could muster. Eventually I surmised that there was more to his megalomaniac behavior, I just had no time to figure it out.

The *him* was Dick Stiverson. He was my boss and the beverage manager. The best way I could describe him was that he looked *peculiar.* He was in his early-thirties and stood around five foot eight, but it was hard to tell because of his perpetual slouch. He was very overweight and was always sweating. He also had bad skin and to top off the look, he wore glasses. Even in a suit, he appeared unkempt and slovenly. He was never friendly or approachable *unless* your position of authority was above his, and there was a constant smirk on his face which made him always look like he was up to no good. But enough about Dick for now.

My name is Alicide Jefferson Porter, but everyone calls me "AJ". *This is my story.*

Chapter 2

I am an Assistant Beverage Manager at The Grand Regency International Hotel & Suites, located in the Inner Harbor of Baltimore, Maryland. I have worked here for almost nine months and although the hospitality industry was new to me at the time, I was a quick study.

The responsibility and profession of taking care of people was pleasurable and rapidly got into my blood. At twenty-seven, I considered myself an easygoing guy and a good man. I am also a former Marine and this job at the Regency was my second job since becoming a civilian.

Today, as usual, I came in a bit early for my shift. I like to get a head start on what needs to be done and get things rolling, but I was now standing in front of Dick's desk with high hopes that what I was saying to him would finally make sense. His response was to become more engrossed in looking at the papers on his desk.

To an outsider, his actions would probably appear genuine but I'd witnessed him doing this before. It was something he did when he wanted to ignore me, so his shuffling of the papers was a ruse. He was only faking like he was completing some administrative task.

When I was first hired, one of the first things I noticed about Dick was that he was lazy, and he proved that over the next eight months I had been here. Unless someone in a higher position was around and possibly watching, he never did much of anything. Right now, he wanted me out of his space, so he continued shuffling papers and then squinted at his computer screen. Adding to the show, occasionally, he'd punch some made-up numbers into a ten-key calculator. I'd have to admit, he had his routine of looking busy down pat. If I walked out of our office right now, his task would be miraculously completed and he would be gone from the hotel without so much as a *kiss my ass*.

I ignored his act and kept standing there in front of his desk, waiting for a response. I liked my newfound career field and refused to be run out of it because someone did not have an open mind, but his actions were beginning to tax my nerves, to say the least.

With a deep sigh I said, "Dick, I'm continuously checking on the event spaces and the beverage outlets during my shifts. If any outlet or the front desk needs me, they just contact me on my pager so the fact that I forgot it is not such a big deal."

Unfortunately he was not someone who was open to new technology and innovation, or I would have shown him the device I had clipped to my belt. It was my personal Iridium Motorola Satellite Pager. I got it while stationed in Japan. I had splurged and purchased it at a Tokyo electronics shop because somehow I knew then that it would come in handy someday.

A little larger than a normal pager, it could receive alphanumeric messages of up to 620 characters on four lines. I could be in a bathhouse in Russia during a thunderstorm or on a sunny beach under a grape tree in Tobago, and I would get your message almost instantly from wherever you were located. As long as I had access to a satellite, it was reachable from anywhere.

When you called my number, you were greeted with a prerecorded message of my voice: "Hi, this is AJ. Sorry, I missed your call. Please press number one to leave a numeric phone number after the beep, or press number two to be transferred to my answering service, which will transcribe and immediately deliver your message to me. Thanks for calling." It was a great tool and never failed me. Albeit three years old from when I purchased it, it was still state of the art. Satellite communication equipment wasn't yet used or widely known in the States, and being able to use it made me feel like I owned a piece of superspy equipment. Today it was still the leading piece of equipment in the field of advanced communication technology.

I knew that showing him this pager would start another argument, so I withheld from demonstrating to him the merits and results I already had while using it here at work.

As Dick continued to shuffle invoices on his desk, he grew more perturbed. It was a pleasant temperature in our office, but he was sweating and his face was red. With an exasperated sigh, he pushed the papers to the side, took off his glasses, and pinched the bridge of his nose.

He then wiped the sweat from his brow, put his glasses back on, turned his head to me, and looked at a spot somewhere above my head.

Another thing about Dick: whenever he deigned to talk to me, he never looked directly at my face. His gaze always hovered just to my right, left, or somewhere above my head. I wondered if he had strabismus—old-fashioned cock-eyed—or if it was me. My eyes change colors depending on my mood, and I'd heard everything from 'captivating' to 'unnatural.' Was he so enamored he couldn't bear to focus? I doubt it. Eventually, I gave up trying to sidestep into his line of sight; whenever I moved, he just found a new spot on the wall to study.

This strange habit perplexed me until one day I saw him interacting with someone else and he looked directly at them, into their eyes. That was when I convinced that he was just a weird asshole and the 'not looking at me' thing was his idea of a villainous disrespect.

He said, "Look, I'm going to tell you this for the last time. That piece of equipment is part of your uniform and your pager is not. Whether or not you think its functional is beside the point. It's what we do here at The Grand Regency International Hotel & Suites and all managers have to wear the full uniform, at all times, when we are on duty. No exceptions!"

I had not planned to get into it with him today, but when I arrived at work, a Verbal Warning was on my desk. My normally lazy boss had made one of his rare outlet inspections and found the bulky radio I'd been carrying the night before sitting on an empty keg in the restaurant's cooler. So, he wrote me up without giving me a chance to explain what had happened.

Chapter 3

The previous evening, I was the closing Manager and no Barbacks were scheduled to work the late shift. From his past tendencies, I knew Dick had purposely not scheduled any one. I had to do a lot of 'schlepping' but I held my own and persevered through the demanding shift. Close to the end of the night, as luck would have it, the bar in the top floor Fine Dining Restaurant ran a beer keg dry so it was my responsibility to get a replacement.

The task of changing a keg in that outlet was not easy. First I had to retrieve a new keg from the warehouse cooler on the hotel's ground floor. Once I got there I loaded the squat, round fifty-five-pound aluminum beast onto a two-wheel dolly and then had to get the bulky payload down the hallway onto the freight elevator to the top floor.

Once on the fifteenth floor, it took maneuvering the keg down a crowded, skinny hallway and entering the back of a fully operating kitchen, dodging cooks and kitchen hazards. When I finally made it safely to the cooler, I had to then take the keg off the dolly and maneuver it through a maze of fruit and vegetable crates and Lexan containers of foodstuffs, sauces, and marinating meats to the keg system along the rear wall.

 Not wanting to sweat out my suit jacket any more than I already had, I took it, and the perpetually silent radio off, and began to work. I disconnected and removed the empty keg, then wrestled with the full keg until I got it into place. Once I got it situated and connected, I double-checked the lines and how it flowed out at the bar. With everything operating correctly, I retrieved my jacket and the dolly holding the empty keg, and exited the cooler. For the rest of my shift I never realized I had left the radio behind.

I wanted to argue more about the write-up, but Dick had dismissed me by once again by ignoring my presence and focusing his attention back to his faking. When my face and ears grew hot, I knew my anger was beginning to boil, so I forced myself to walk away.

As I made my way to the walkie-talkie charging station I heard him say, "By the way, AJ, I understand that you instructed the Barbacks and Bartenders to throw away the empty liquor bottles. Stop it immediately! I want those bottles kept so I can track the usage versus distribution levels of each outlet. Do you think you can handle that or do I need to make you understand some other way?"

That stopped me in my tracks. Rooted to the spot it took me a couple seconds to grasp what I had just heard. It was as if he was daring me to say something back to him. He didn't realize how close I was to barring the door so no one would interrupt us, then inviting him to show me what he was really trying to say. Luckily for both of us, without even acknowledging him, I grabbed a radio, powered it on, checked the channel, clipped it to my belt, and headed out of the office.

When the door shut behind me I swear I heard him chuckling.

If I had another job prospect in the wings, that last jab might have gone another way entirely but the main reason I walked away before things escalated was that if the situation did intensify into a physical confrontation, it would not have be a fair fight. Why? Because Dick only had one functional arm. Unless he had some sort of weapon secreted close by, he didn't stand a chance against me.

Waiting for the freight elevator, I realized that Dick reminded me a little of a man I was in the Corps with, Sergeant Al Smith. He was a muscle bound, loud, narcissistic bully who led through terror. At six foot four and 250 pounds, he bragged about his fighting and killing skills. He thrived on disrespecting subordinates until a young Marine finally stood up to him.

That day they stripped off their blouses to remove their rank, but before Smith could even pull his arm from his sleeve, the kid shattered his nose with a left jab and followed it up with a right cross. When Smith woke up he requested a transfer, and reportedly became the nicest guy at his new duty station.

I smiled, knowing that one day, Dick would disrespect the wrong person and his disability wouldn't save him from a similar fate.

Chapter 4

As the elevator rose, I recalled the rumors about how "Lazy Dick" lost that arm.

Two years prior, he was a fresh Hospitality Management graduate hired as an assistant supervisor for the hotel's three-meal bistro. Even then, management dubbed him "Lazy Dick," a low-energy snitch and shameless sycophant.
At the time, the Regency was thriving; two quarters of rising occupancy and 98% guest satisfaction had finally triggered performance bonuses. To celebrate, the owners hosted an off-site happy hour—a rare chance for the team to unwind, indulge in top-shelf liquor, and feast on hors d'oeuvres.

 Department supervisors had not been invited because they were on duty, overseeing the hotel in their managers' absence, but after closing the food and beverage outlets, Dick crashed the party uninvited.

Though unwelcome, the managers allowed him stay and in an attempt to catch up to everyone's two-hour consumption head start, Dick quickly got himself incredibly drunk.

At the end of the night, with his body now full of alcohol and possibly some recreational drugs, he made the poor decision to drive himself home. Although several managers saw him staggering out of the venue with his car keys in hand, no one offered a safer alternative.

It was a rainy night, and Dick's level of impairment, combined with poor driving conditions resulted in a crash that left the car unrecognizable and Dick near death. Thrown through the windshield after neglecting his seatbelt, he was found by State Troopers.

As paramedics rushed him to shock trauma, the troopers used his Regency access card to alert hotel security. The hotel's HR executive contacted his parents in rural Frostburg who immediately raced toward Baltimore, praying their son would still be alive when they arrived.

Dick's toxicology report confirmed a lethal cocktail of alcohol, cocaine, and a ketamine and while he lay in a medically induced coma, surgeons worked feverishly to stabilize his breathing, repair shattered bones, and stem the internal bleeding.

They saved his life, but his right arm was a lost cause. With the nerves irreparably shredded, doctors urged his parents to authorize an amputation while Dick was still unconscious. Despite offers of state-of-the-art prosthetics, his parents now blinded by the prospect of a massive lawsuit settlement, refused to approve the removal of the arm so, like Humpty Dumpty, the doctors stitched him back together as best they could.

His lawyers secured an out-of-court settlement that covered all medical expenses and guaranteed Dick's indefinite employment—a quiet payoff to bury the scandal.

Through grueling physical therapy, Dick eventually relearned to walk, but he was forced to adapt to a new reality: navigating life as a left-hander with a useless, withered limb hanging at his side. Four months later, he returned to the Regency as Beverage Manager, a role he was utterly unqualified for but legally insulated within.

The accident hadn't humbled him but had weaponized his narcissism. Dick became an arrogant, verbally abusive "Teflon Don," shielded from consequences by the hotel's fear of litigation. He treated subordinates with open contempt, knowing that even the most egregious complaints would result in nothing more than a wrist slap.

Behind his back, the staff traded his old nickname for a new one: "Swinging Lefty." Without a sling or his left hand to steady it, his dead right arm flailed wildly as he walked—a pathetic, rhythmic pendulum I was forced to witness daily. Even more jarring was the heavy, wet thud it made when he'd drop it onto his desk to serve as a macabre paperweight. It was exhausting just to watch. I could only imagine the physical toll of lugging that useless weight around all day.

<u>*Chapter 5*</u>

Leaning on the back of the elevator wall, I retreated into thoughts of karma as we ascended, watching coworkers filter out floor by floor. Sometimes, the civilian world felt like a minefield of "potholes" I hadn't yet learned to navigate. I missed the Corps. As an active Marine, I knew exactly how to handle a threat, but here, the rules of engagement were frustratingly unclear.

A quick trip to the recruiter is all it would take, but with the latest conflict escalating, reenlisting meant an inevitable return to the desert. I'd be forcing myself back into a world where killing was expected. I wasn't afraid of the work, but I dreaded the cost: the nightmares and the creeping PTSD.

Luck had spared me from taking a life during my two enlistments, but I'd come hauntingly close in Beirut. I was part of the 1,300-strong response force sent in after a suicide bomber drove a 12,000-pound truck bomb into the barracks. It was a deadly Sunday morning; while the city slept, the blast leveled the building, claiming 241 American lives.

My unit was ordered in to secure the area and recover the wounded and the fallen. To this day, responsibility remains a subject of debate, though the Islamic Jihad Organization—widely considered a front for Hezbollah—claimed the attack with Iranian backing. Rumors of CIA involvement still circulate as "scuttlebutt," but the cost was undeniably clear: 220 Marines, 18 Sailors, and 3 Soldiers were killed. Including the driver, 242 lives were extinguished in an instant.

Forty-eight hours after the blast, my unit was sorting through the rubble. For the next seven days, we recovered bodies and fragments—a duty fueled by grief and a simmering, dangerous rage. I spent every shift with my M16 locked, loaded, and my finger hovering over the trigger, desperate for a target.

We dreamed of revenge, but our guerrilla adversaries had vanished. In my mind, they hadn't run but simply melted back into the populace, resuming their lives as if they hadn't just ended hundreds of ours.

I know now I'm better off for never finding a target, but back then, I was ready to kill anyone I could blame. I've had to learn that even in service to your country, killing is still killing, and the label of 'murderer' doesn't just wash off. It's not like the movies; you can try to drown your guilt in alcohol or narcotics, but those ghosts never leave.

The elevator doors slid open at my floor, snapping me back to reality. I stepped out, realizing that even with an asshole boss like "Swinging Lefty," the civilian world was a far better place to be.

My first stop was the Bistro Bar—the Regency's *problem child* location. A 165-seat three-meal restaurant with a cramped, six-seat bar, it served overpriced, mediocre fare to unimpressed guests.

This was also Dick's personal dungeon. If you crossed him, he'd tuck you away here to rot. With dismal tips and a revolving door of disgruntled staff, the Bistro was where new hires were sent to prove their worth—or break. Nobody worked this outlet by choice.

Tonight's sacrificial lamb was "Miss Theresa," a Black woman in her mid-fifties who clung to heavy makeup and a rotating collection of youthful wigs. Today's choice was a blonde up-do that sat crooked on her head. Dick had banished her from the lucrative banquet circuit months ago after a run-in with one of his sycophants. Now, she was stuck here, retaliated against and counting pennies in the Bistro.

I found her perched on a stool, shoes kicked off, popping gum over a paperback. She was so deep in her book she didn't notice me until I cleared my throat. Startled, she snapped the book shut and jammed her feet back into her shoes.

"Oh, hey hon. How you doin'?"

"I'm good, Theresa. Everything going alright?"

"Slow as usual but my back is flaring up today. I was hoping someone would help get Miss Theresa some ice for the bin. Can you help? I'd really appreciate it."

I considered refusing the "Miss Theresa" bait, but let it slide. I grabbed a five-gallon bucket and headed for the kitchen. It took me three trips to the ice machine to fill her bin, hauling the weight across the floor while she watched.

While I hauled ice, Theresa aired her grievances—blaming Dick for her aching back and the lack of banquet hours. I tuned her out, mentally cataloging the bar's unfinished side work, which only made her switch tactics. Digging a pen under her wig to scratch an itch, she leaned in with a toxic rumor.

"You know, hon, I heard Dick and that front desk supervisor talking and laughing about you the other day. I was making my cash drop when I heard 'Lefty' say you weren't nothing. He told her you must be some affirmative action hire—useless and inexperienced."

I kept my expression unreadable as I set down the final bucket, refusing to give her the reaction she was fishing for.

"Thanks for the information, Theresa. I'll keep it in mind." My tone didn't shift as I pivoted from the gossip to the job. "However, there are a few things I need from you now, or I'll have to write you up."

I pointed to her feet. "Keep your shoes on. It's a hygiene issue, a safety violation, and very unprofessional."

Next, I gestured toward the stool. "That can't be out here so it has to go back to the storage room."

She obeyed, returning to the bar with a sour look.

"Also, I know it's quiet but if you have time to read, please find a way to do it out of sight. And the gum - Lose it. I heard you popping from across the room."

She immediately put it in a napkin and threw it in the trash.

I offered one final glance around. "If you need help, please call a bar back—that's what they're there for."

I walked out, repulsed by her petty tattling, even if it was about Dick. I don't trust snitches, but I didn't doubt her story.

Chapter 6

As I descending the red-carpeted stairs toward the Grand Constellation Ballroom, I weighed Theresa's words while nodding to passing guests. I knew Dick had a target on my back, but I couldn't pin down a motive. It would have been easy to chalk it up to racial bias, but I'd watched him long enough to know his malice was non-discriminatory; he was just as shitty to the white staff.

Dick was a narcissist who hated anyone he couldn't control. I knew that my military leadership, not a quota, got me through the door but to kill that overdressed schlepper perception, I had to prove my value, and fast.

I took a sharp, cleansing breath, shoved the gossip into a dark corner of my mind, and stepped into the banquet hall to check on my team.

A Bar Mitzvah was in full swing, with two hundred guests divided into two distinct worlds. On the adult side, three mobile bars boasted every kosher liquor imaginable; guests drank, flirted, and brokered business deals through a haze of laughter and smoke.

Across the room, a chaotic swarm of children ran and screamed, leaving a trail of wasted food and spilled drinks. The two camps existed in perfect, mutual ignorance.

I hung back, remaining a ghost at the edge of the room. Experience had taught me that staying invisible was the best way to see how the staff truly operated when they weren't performing for a manager.

There were 3 bars staffed at this event. After a few minutes of observation, I drifted toward the martini bar. Frank, a seasoned veteran, was diligently managing the crowd, so I gave him a silent nod of approval and moved on. On the children's side, Luzira was essentially playing babysitter between pouring sodas; seeing she had her hands full with the chaos, I circled back toward the main event corridor.

The second liquor bar was manned by Jessie, a guy in his thirties who'd always been solid. I pulled up beside him, and we both took in the spectacle.

"Man, I wish my parents had thrown me a party like this when I turned thirteen."

Jessie snorted. "Where would you have found this many friends? Besides, these are Bawl'more Jews—you know the ducats they're dropping tonight is chump change to them. A party like this would've broken my people and yours too."

I flashed a grin. "You got that right."

I scanned the room for the third bar, eventually spotting it tucked so deep into the corner that guests would have to trek across the ballroom to utilize it. Manning that isolated station was Bob, a big white guy that I avoided most times. He was a mediocre bartender at best, yet somehow he consistently landed the highest-earning shifts. I knew from previous events that the placement was wrong, but again, I held back to observe.

I watched as he worked the shadows of the Grand Constellation Ballroom, wondering who had authorized the move. After ten minutes, Bob hadn't served a soul—until a couple made the long walk to his corner. When the guest laid a few bills on the bar, Bob didn't drop them in the communal tip jar as required by all staff; he palmed the cash and stuffed it straight into his back pocket, a blatant violation of our pooled gratuity policy.

Then, as bold as if he were a customer, Bob reached under the counter, drained a rocks glass, and casually mixed himself a fresh Absolut and Lime. He smacked his lips in approval and tucked his contraband cocktail back out of sight. I couldn't believe the balls on this guy. Between the theft, the drinking on duty, and a missing tie from his uniform, Bob was a walking HR disaster.

I moved across the room to his bar, avoiding guests as they enjoyed themselves. As I closed the distance between us, our eyes locked, and Bob snapped into a stiff, professional like posture. I stepped behind the bar and stood right next to him, looking out at the guests. I didn't say a word, just stared out into the ballroom, letting the silence do the heavy lifting. I can tell that he was visibly twitching, stealing glances at me and inching away as though my silence felt like a noose.

Finally, the pressure cracked him. Turning to me he said, "Can I do something for you, AC?"
I turned and looked him dead in the face.

"What did you call me?"

"Huh?" was all he could muster.

I pointed at my name badge, staring into his bloodshot eyes.

"What. Is. My. Name?"

He leaned in, squinting sheepishly at the tag and replied. "Oh, sorry... AJ."

"I don't need anything from you right now, Bob," I said, my voice cold. "But we'll talk later."

Outside of the ballroom, the silence in the hallway was a sharp contrast to the party's roar. I finished my rounds and hurried back to the office. Before I could make a report of my finding I had to follow protocol. I called Dick's home and got no answer. His answering machine did not even kick on. I then paged him and waited for a response, but my managerial due diligence was met with silence.

As time passed it was clear that Dick was not going to contact me back, so I made a decision. If Dick wasn't going to lead, I was going to follow the book. I opened Dick's desk bottom drawer where he kept a copy of our HR Manual with all Protocol and Procedures guidelines, and was shocked at what I found.

Chapter 7

The drawer revealed a space that also doubled as a den of unprofessionalism and potential corruption.

Alongside two pornographic magazines: an edition of *Hustler* and a well-worn copy of *Big White Butts,* there was a spiral notebook that hinted at some sort of scheme. There were initials, abbreviations, and a list of escalating dollar figures. Even more alarming was the stack of unofficial manila folders that held personal "shadow files" on many employees. In each folder were copies of official applications, emergency contact forms, verbal and written warnings, and dates of call offs and tardiness.

I was not sure why Dick would have or need this information but he made his thoughts about each person known through the handwritten scribblings of his personal opinion. The majority of his judgments were highly negative and unprofessional. The most positive of them had nothing to do with work, but were instead descriptions of current and former female associates' physiques.

When I saw the folder with Bob's names on it, I had to look. It was the smoking gun. Unlike the others, his disciplinary forms were the originals, not copies—stashed away so they officially didn't exist. By all rights, his mountain of infractions should have gotten him fired years ago.

Then I saw that his emergency contact had Dick's name and number, with "1ST CUZIN" scribbled next to it. His audacity made sense now; Bob wasn't just bold, he was protected. The realization that Dick was running the department like a private fiefdom, shielding family while burying the rest of us, had my blood boiling.

I had seen enough for now. I located what I needed and flipped to the sections on theft of gratuities and on-duty intoxication. I was stunned as I read the termination rules.

The HR Manual was absolute: any alcohol or drug use required on-the-spot termination and immediate removal from the property. I started to feel good. I guess I could go back up to the bar and fire him, but as I continued reading, that good feeling evaporated. Company policy also required a second manager or a security officer to witness any termination so my options were bleak.

The security team was notoriously lazy, avoiding anything that wasn't a major crime. That left only the Front Desk Supervisor on duty tonight—the very same woman Theresa had heard giggling with Dick as he trashed my reputation. Seeking her help was out of the question. She was clearly in Dick's pocket so I was trapped between a corporate mandate I'd already stalled on and a witness pool that was either incompetent or hostile. By failing to act, I'd potentially handed Dick the very fuel he needed to fire me.

There had to be something I could do so I started building a different kind of case. If I couldn't get him for drinking and stealing, I'd bury him in paperwork.

I drafted written warnings for his missing tie and substandard performance, then tacked on verbal citations for mishandling tips, service failures, and health code violations. I double-checked my spelling, made three copies, and mentally rehearsed my speech, ready to turn the screws. I couldn't fire him tonight, but I was betting Bob didn't know that.

When the banquet bars rolled in I started the inventory of each cart, intentionally saving Bob for last. I could feel his eyes on me, and I didn't miss his impatient mumble to Luzira:

"I wish he'd hurry the hell up. I got someplace to be!"

I played it cool, acting like I hadn't heard a word, but my military training kept him in my peripheral vision. That's how I caught him sliding a backpack from under his bar and ducking into the men's locker room. When he emerged a few minutes later, the bag was gone.

With the other bartenders now gone, it was just Bob and me. I took my time, stunned to find the same glass he'd been drinking from still sitting under the bar—he hadn't even bothered to hide the evidence.

As I meticulously counted his inventory, he groaned. "Can we hurry this up? Dick never takes this long, and he ain't gonna be happy about the extra time on the clock."

"Don't you worry about that," I replied flatly. Once the count was finished, I signaled toward the door. "Step into the office for a minute. I want to talk to you."

He was wary but followed, standing stiffly in front of my desk. I entered the office behind him, closing the distance and taking his measure—just in case this went south.

Bob stood an inch taller than me, a six-foot-two frame that looked more like a Longshoreman than a bartender. Despite his 220 pounds, my memory of him in the locker room—clad only in boxers and socks—revealed the truth: he was a soft collection of a beer belly, man-boobs, and love handles so, yeah, he was big, sure, but it was mostly unconditioned mass.

Chapter 8

"Have a seat, Bob." He sank into the chair, the bravado starting to leak out. "Earlier tonight, I saw you drinking, and don't bother," I added, cutting him off with a raised hand. "The glass you used is sitting right under your bar."

"I was just drinkin' ice water," he whined, his voice thin for a man his size.

"You're lying! I watched you drain that glass, top it off with Absolut, and add a squeeze of lime. I watched you drink that one, too."

I leaned in, letting the silence of the office press against him. The "ice water" excuse was a joke, and we both knew it.

The wheels were turning in his head, but his defense was stalling. I stepped into the hallway, retrieved the glass from beneath his bar, and set it on the desk between us like a piece of evidence. The Absolut and lime scent was still fresh in the glass. Bob stared at it, then at me.

"In addition to drinking," I continued, my voice dropping an octave, "I watched you palm cash tips and slide them into your pocket instead of the communal jar. So, on top drinking on the job, you're a thief."

He was either a gifted actor or genuinely terrified because his eyes welled up, and his Adam's apple bobbed as he struggled for air.

"So am I fired? Does Dick know?" He began to cry silently, wiping tears from his cheeks. Seeing a man his size break down like that was disconcerting—it was embarrassing to watch the "big, bad" persona evaporate into a weeping mess.

I let him sit in his emotional collapse for a moment, the power dynamic in the room shifting entirely. He wasn't the protected "first cousin" anymore; he was a caught thief.

I spun the HR Manual around, pinning my finger to the bolded paragraph on the Regency's Drug & Alcohol Policy. I watched his bloodshot eyes scan the words: *Immediate termination and removal from the property.*

"You see what this says, Bob. It says that you should be out on the street ten minutes ago." I let the weight of the corporate mandate sink in as he stared at the grounds for dismissal.

"Read this section please. It's the same one you agreed to and signed when you were hired."

As he looked down, his mouth moved as if he were struggling to sound out the letters. The words seemed to confuse him, and a realization hit me: Was Bob illiterate? It was painful to watch, so I read the statement for him: "Employees are prohibited from eating or drinking in operational areas. Possession, suspicion of being under the influence, or consumption of alcohol or drugs is grounds for immediate discharge."

I flipped three pages forward while Bob watched, his expression vacant. "Bartenders and servers will pool all tips," I read, my voice steady. "Gratuities are distributed evenly by hours worked." I finished by reciting the policies on personal grooming and uniform standards.

Bob stared at the desk, sniffled loudly, and swallowed. Finally, he reached into his pocket, pulled out a crumpled wad of cash, and dropped it between us.

"That's all I took," he mumbled, his "1st Cuzin" bravado completely extinguished.

The theft was now a confession, and the money sat there as physical evidence of his dishonesty.

I counted the thirteen dollars, shaking my head in disgust. "You risked your job for *this*?" I dropped the measly bills into the tip envelope with the rest of the night's earnings.

I slid the paperwork across the desk. "These are three verbal warnings. One for drinking in guest areas, one for the uniform violation, and one for improper tip handling." I leaned in, my voice dropping. "I didn't mention the Absolut or the theft. I just wrote that you were 'drinking something' and 'mishandling cash.' If there's a next time, I'm putting it all in writing."

Bob stared at the forms, the reality of his narrow escape finally sinking in. He knew I'd just handed him a lifeline he didn't deserve—and that I now owned him.

I slid the forms across the desk. "Sign and date all six copies. One for you, one for Dick, and one for HR."

As he stood to leave, stammering his thanks, I barked, "Sit back down! We're not finished." I leaned in, letting the air out of his relief. "I cut you a break tonight but if I catch even a hint of shade from you again, I'll have a witness ready and you'll be gone before you can blink. Do you understand?"

"Yeah," he mumbled. "I understand."

I handed him his copies and dismissed him with a cold, "You can go."

He slunk out without another word. I left Dick's copies squarely on his desk for him to see in the morning and sealed the final set in an envelope for the HR Director. The paper trail was set.

Chapter 9

While Bob and I were having our tête-à-tête, the rest of the outlets closed. I spent the next hour on security checks and cleanliness inspections before returning to the office to draft my manager's action report.

As I typed, I wondered what kind of hell Dick would raise once he realized I'd disciplined his family member. I doubted Bob would be stupid enough to complain to HR about my "lenient" write-ups, but I braced for the inevitable blowback. Whatever was coming, the milk was already spilled; I'd officially declared war on Dick's private fiefdom.

I closed up shop and stepped into the Baltimore night air. Tomorrow was my day off, and my only mission was catching last call at a bar around the corner.

At 12:30 a.m., the Inner Harbor was still humming, but the tourists were now outnumbered by criminal opportunists. I scanned the sidewalks, seeing pickpockets, roving bands of kids looking for trouble, and the late-shift dealers and streetwalkers staking out their corners. The "workday" for the city's underbelly was just getting started.

I reached Barnacle Bill's Seafood Emporium a block away, managing to run the gauntlet of panhandlers and street dealers without being hassled. It was a corny name for a bar, but the drinks were stiff and the kitchen was solid. I'd first found the place the day I signed my contract at the Regency Suites, and it had been my sanctuary ever since.

I claimed a stool at the bar and ordered the crab cakes with slaw and fries. While I waited, I settled in with a double shot of Old Crow, a pint of National Bohemian, and a glass of water to wash away the shift.

As I ate, two attractive women in nurses' scrubs took the stools next to me—one blonde, the other Black with her dreadlocks wrapped in a scarf. The Black woman leaned past her friend and asked, "Excuse me, but will it bother you if we smoke?"

I shook my head and went back to my food. They settled in, the smell of clove or menthol soon mixing with the scent of Old Crow and crab cakes. It was a typical Baltimore mix—night-shift workers decompressing after a long haul, just like me.

When the bartender delivered their rounds, I saw they were on the same program—shot and a beer. I ordered another for myself and decided to cast a line. "Ladies, if you let me get a refill, I'll join you in a shot, if you don't mind."

Blondie didn't just decline; she sneered. "Who said we wanted to drink with you? We don't know you."

The air at the bar suddenly felt as cold as the Natty Boh in my hand. Her hostility was sharp, a jagged contrast to the relaxed post-shift vibe I was chasing. I didn't let the brush-off phase me. I pushed my plate aside, flashed my best smile, and extended a hand. "Sorry about that—I'm AJ. Now you know me."

The Black lady reached across, giving me a firm, military-grade handshake. "I'm Ronelle, but my friends call me Ronnie, and this is Carrie, and we'd love to drink with you. Carrie rolled her eyes, offering me only her fingertips like I was a chore.

When the rounds arrived, we tapped glass. "Ronnie and Carrie, nice to meet you," I toasted. "Here's to your health and your wealth."

We knocked back the shots, wincing as the burn hit, then reached for our chasers. Carrie slammed her hand on the bar, the earlier frost finally melting. "Goddamn, I needed that! Let's do another!"

Ronnie shot her a warning look. "Alright, girl, but remember last time? You were hungover for two days. Better pace yourself."

"Ssshiitt," Carrie scoffed, waving for the bartender. "I'll be fine. I ain't no lightweight!"

The night was shifting from a quiet post-work wind-down into something more volatile. As the bartender headed back our way, I wondered if I was about to watching a slow-motion train wreck.

We were all drinking for the same reason—the kind of post-shift exhaustion that only heavy pours can dull. Ronnie and I kept the conversation moving as she told me they were nurses at the Baltimore VA Medical Center, but Carrie remained a wall of "hmphs" and teeth-sucking.

When I mentioned I was new to the city and buried in work, Carrie cut me off with a sharp, "If you got it going on like you say, what you doin' in here alone?"

It didn't win her over, but the eye-rolling finally stopped. Ronnie, meanwhile, was doing her talking with her eyes, flirting with me over the rim of her glass. I excused myself to the restroom for a minute and when I returned, they were gone.

Chapter 10

The next day, I awoke at six thirty a.m. with only a slight hangover. I sat on the edge of the bed acclimating myself to the new day. I smiled as I remembered the night before. I definitely hoped I'd see Ronnie in there again soon.

I started coffee, poured some OJ, and let mellow reggae set the mood while I prepped breakfast. I whisked eggs with a splash of half-and-half, water, and a dice of tomatoes, onions, and jalapeños. Once the butter sizzled in the skillet, I poured the mixture in, eventually folding in crumbled leftover crab. Ten minutes later, I was eating breakfast.

Sitting in the patio garden having a smoke and some coffee, I thought about how lucky I was to have found this apartment. The rent was affordable with water and gas included, and it was only a short commute to work. Though, I did have two faults with the place.

One annoyance was the approach. To get home, I had to round the block, hang two rights, and head down an alley to a heavy wooden door guarded by three deadbolts. Only then did I reach the garden patio leading to my front door.

The second drawback was the lack of insulation, heat, or AC. It was manageable in the spring, but winter promised to be brutal.

My ground-floor unit was a repurposed storage space, tucked beneath three floors of apartments occupied by art students. Though they had access to the patio via an iron staircase, they never seemed to use it. It felt like my private sanctuary, an extension of my living room that I eventually planned to beautify with string lights and potted flowers.

Above me I could hear the girls moving about, getting ready to head out for the day. It was about nine fifteen, and within an hour or so, they'd be gone and the house would be empty.

My reverie was interrupted when my phone rang. I didn't feel like moving so I let my answering machine get it. I heard Dick's voice say, "Uh, hey AJ. This is Dick. I know its short notice, but ah, I wanted to see if you would switch shifts with me today. I'm not feeling good. Call me back please."

After a while, I replayed the message, and he sounded more drunk than sick. I mumbled to the answering machine, "Motherfucker, you must be crazy!" but then contemplated on his request. Keeping in mind that this was the same guy who'd been dogging me for months, I couldn't believe he was asking me for a favor. If I did him a solid and traded shifts with him, would it lead to a positive turning point in our relationship? Heck no it won't! I quickly made a decision. I deleted his message and unplugged the phone. Fuck him! I had things on my schedule today.

After a hot shower, I left the apartment to visit the hardware store around the corner. I bought an electric jigsaw, four adjustable air vent grills, a roll of aluminum tape, a roll of duct tape, a tube of white caulk, and five cans of white spray paint. Next door was a consignment shop, where I bought a used electric heater with a blower, a round crystal ashtray, a stack of comics, and a policeman's black leather sap. Back home, making certain my housemates were gone, I got to work.

The building's main ductwork ran right across my ceiling. I traced the vents onto the metal and carefully cut four openings. I slotted the grills in, sealed the edges with tape and caulk, and finished the whole run with a fresh coat of white spray paint. I stepped back, impressed; for an amateur job, it looked professional. From now on, whenever the girls turned on the air conditioning or heat upstairs, I was going to get some too.

I cleaned up my construction pieces, ran the vacuum, and was about to take out the trash when I noticed something written on the takeout bag I threw in the trashcan. Written in purple ink was a note that read: *You should give me a call sometime, Ronnie.* There was also a number with a winking smiley face. I laughed and high-fived myself as I took out the trash. It was going to be a good day! I had pulled off some MacGyver-type construction and got a chick's number without even trying. Not wanting to appear too eager, I'll let her wait a day or two before I called her.

I loaded a duffle bag with dirty clothes, secured the apartment, and headed across the alley to the laundry mat in the North Avenue strip mall. As I walked, the landscape changed drastically and suddenly. Bolton Hill was gentrified, renovated, and mostly White-yuppie occupied, but the neighborhood across the street looked grimy, urban-tinged, and was definitely a poor neighborhood. The strip mall housed the laundromat, a carry out/liquor store, pawnshop, Chinese restaurant, an ancient-looking grocery store, a store-front Holiness church, and what was now a boarded-up Rite Aid drugstore.

<u>**Chapter 11**</u>

At the entrance to the laundromat, I said good morning to two elderly ladies seated in chairs outside the door. One was heavyset, at least 250 pounds, and the other was barely a hundred pounds. Next to them were neatly folded clothes stacked in baskets. They barely grunted a greeting in return and eyed me with suspicion. When I entered the building, I took a quick look around and noted the other customers waiting on laundry or folding clothes. I located some empty washers, loaded them up, and hid my duffle bag under a table.

The two ladies outside laughed and chatted, but when I approached, they went silent. I sat on the edge of the sidewalk a few feet away and lit a cigarette. As I watched the movements of the neighborhood, I could feel the eyes of the ladies on me, but I ignored them. Suddenly a voice said, "Excuse me, Officer!"

I looked around to see where a policeman might be, when another voice chimed in: "She's talkin' to you, Officer."

When I turned in their direction, they were both looking at me. "Excuse me, ma'am?"

"You the police," The slimmer one said. "Are you working?"

"Ma'am, I'm not a policeman," I answered.

The other lady, grinned and sucked her teeth. "Well, baby, if you ain't the po-lice, you sure look like one."

I was a bit insulted they thought I was the police and was about to say something, but before I could get a word out, she continued, "Well, we ain't doin' nothing illegal, but you know you supposed to tell us if you the police, if we ask you."

I was about to say that I was not a plain-clothes officer when the thin lady added, "Well, if you ain't po-lice, I know you ain't from 'round here."

"No ma'am, I'm not from here, but I live across the street. I'm just doing my laundry. What, are y'all two, the neighborhood watch or something?"

Like they had practiced this act before they both rolled their eyes. Holding up an index finger the big lady said. "One, again, you look like the po-lice."

And, then the thin woman said, while holding up two fingers, "And two … well, son, you standing out." When she finished all three of us laughed.

At that moment I realized what they might be seeing in me. "Well, I recently got out of the Marine Corps, but like I said, I ain't the police. I work in a hotel."

"See girl, I told you he reminded me of James." She looked at me and said, "James is my ex-husband, and he was in Vietnam. He came home and wasn't right in the head, so I divorced his crazy ass. Dem shell-shock nightmares and using that crack got him lost out there in these streets somewhere, or he dead."

"We weren't tryin' to insult you, but you do got a look about you. You say you live over there across the street?"

"Yes ma'am. You can almost see my patio straight over there. Why?"

"I'll give you some advice. Dee's dope boys is hot out here when the sun goes down and if they figure out you ain't the police, they'll rob you or worse. I recommend you stay on that side of the street after dark. The only thing over here during that time, is trouble."

Facing them, I smiled. "Ladies, I appreciate the warning, but I work mostly at night and spend most of my days sleeping. Plus, I've walked over here after dark before to get some carryout without any problem. This ain't the first hood I ever been in, and as for those young cats, they can only kill me one time and I'm hell to catch if I'm scared and get to running."

That earned a giggle from both of them. I excused myself to grab a drink, offering to get them something as well, but they both declined.
As I stepped into the store, a voice drifted in behind me. "Girl, dem Marines got good manners, but I bet you—just like James—he's crazy as batshit underneath." Their laughter followed me down the aisle.

When I returned, the two ladies were being loaded into a car by a young man, and then they were gone. I swapped my laundry to the dryers and headed back outside for a smoke.

My mind drifted back to Dick—I wondered what happened after I dodged his call and how he'd react to Bob's write-ups. Dick had burned through three assistant managers in eighteen months. He'd orchestrated the firing of two for "poor performance" and tormented the third until she quit and fled the state. He was notoriously vindictive toward his assistants, and I knew I was next on deck.

Once my clothes were dry, I folded them, packed my duffle, and headed home. I fixed a quick meal and, as night fell, locked up the apartment and called it a night.

Chapter 12

My alarm buzzed, jolting me into the day. I stretched, offered a quick word of thanks for the morning, and was out the door and on a city bus by 8:07 a.m. My plan was simple: get in early and knock out my opening duties before Dick arrived. The ride was smooth and the bus half-empty until we hit a dead stop—an accident a block ahead had paralyzed traffic in both directions.

I wasn't due until ten, but time was ticking away. I exited the bus and hiked past the wreckage to flag a taxi. One cabbie slowed, but then gunned it away without stopping. I waved down another, yelling a loud "Yo!" The driver pulled ahead and stopped, but as my hand reached for the door handle, he flipped his "Off Duty" sign and peeled away. What the hell was going on? If I weren't so worried about the time, the absurdity would have been funny. This morning, it was just infuriating.

I'd heard the stories of cabbies bypassing Black passengers across the country. Now, the "crime" of being light but not white was stopping me from getting to work.

After muttering a few choice curses at cabbies and their lineage, I started walking. Anything was better than standing there looking like a fool. I'd only made it a block when a green Honda Accord that was traveling in the opposite direction spotted me. The driver pulled a wild U-turn across four lanes and jerked to the curb. He leaned over, peering through the passenger window with a grin.

"You need a ride, brother?"

I silently thanked the universe for Gypsy cabs and climbed into the front seat without a second thought. "Thanks, man," I said, finally feeling the pressure of the clock ease up.

The driver was brown-skinned and the car smelled heavily of pine, but it was clean. A Radio Shack car phone was bolted to the console, and the stereo blared a talk radio station filled with shouting voices. I gave him the address, and he gave me a knowing look.

"The cabbies wouldn't stop for you, huh?"

I stared out the window, the frustration bubbling back up. "Yeah. After the first two, I figured out it was some color shit. How can a city be sixty-five percent Black and the cab drivers still be this prejudiced?"

He let out a dry laugh while weaving through traffic with practiced ease. "It ain't about the math, brother, it's about the mindset. With the livery industry unregulated, they can do whatever they want."

 A few minutes later, he pulled up to the back of the hotel and handed me a card that read *Excelsior Transport, Driver.*

He smiled. "Give me a call if you ever need a ride. If I'm out working, I'll always pick you up." I thanked him, paid my fare, and he sped off into the traffic.

At the associate entrance, I flashed my identification card to activate the turnstile, and as I passed through, the glass window of the security office slid open. Inside was a white guy sitting behind a desk in a crumpled-looking blue suit.

"Excuse me, you are AJ right?"

'Yeah, I'm AJ. How can I help you?'

The man got up from the desk. "I'm Sean-Robert McGillicuddy. I'm the chief of hotel security.

Retired Baltimore Police. If you've got a minute, I'd like to show you something."

"Sure." I said, wondering why he threw in the police part. Following him into the security offices, I speculated what had happened that the head of hotel security could want to talk to me about.

He led me to a command center walled with two dozen monitors. A skinny tech sat at the console, eyes glued to the feeds. McGillicuddy tapped his shoulder. "Mike, take five." The guy grabbed his smokes and cleared out.

McGillicuddy gestured to the empty chair. Once I sat, he cut to the chase. "We caught your staff doing some questionable things on your shift the other night."

He paused, fishing for a reaction from me. When I gave none and stayed silent, he turned to one of the monitors. "Take a look."

I braced myself for footage of Bob pocketing tips at the bar mitzvah, but the screen flickered to the Bistro Bar. The video was silent but sharp. It showed Miss Theresa reading before I arrived. He fast-forwarded to me entering the frame, hauling ice back and forth while she chatted away. He fast-forwarded to the moment I finished with the ice then it stopped. I waited for the rest of the video to show, but it was blank. A cold knot tightened in my gut.

"I wanted you to see this before I hand it to Dick," he said. "He'll decide how to proceed."

I stared, baffled. "Proceed with what? And where's the rest of the footage?"

He looked me dead in the eye. "This is all there is. You need to manage your people better."

He stood, ejected the tape, and scribbled on the label with a marker. I turned my attention to the wall of monitors. I'd always known the cameras were there, but seeing them live in motion—associates and guests being tracked in real-time—was different.

My eyes landed on the Grand Constellation Ballroom. Six angles captured the banquet crew prepping for the next event. Then I spotted it: a lens aimed directly at where Bob's bar had been during the bar mitzvah. The realization hit me. Between the edited tape and the strategic camera angles, I wasn't just being watched—I was being targeted.

Chapter 13

I walked out before he could get another word in, but I could feel the ex-cop's stare boring into my back. In the office, I tried to shake off the encounter, but the "what-ifs" kept looping. I needed to focus. I took a few deep breaths to clear the static, pushed McGillicuddy out of my mind, and got to work.

Today was my first time flying solo on the department payroll, a task Dick usually handled. I knew this was a test of my competence and if I didn't complete it 100% correct and submit it on time, it would give my boss fuel for his fire.

I was nearly done when two red flags popped up. First, Dick had manually entered 55hours for Bob, yet the time clock recorded only 25. Even with overtime, which he didn't work, the math didn't add up. Then things got weirder.

30hours were logged for someone named Mike Essex. I'd never heard the name before, and there was no one with that name in our department.

To stay on schedule, I processed the payroll for the entire department—minus the phantom 30hours for "Essex" and Bob's extra 30. I printed four copies and went to the administrative offices to beat the deadline.

As I dropped the reports in the bins and grabbed the mail, I realized I'd forgotten my radio again. I hurried back, relieved to find Dick still hadn't arrived.

I sat down and fired off an email to Dick about my findings and made an entry in the manager's log, keeping it professional. I explained that I'd excluded the unknown employee since I couldn't find him on any schedule, and I'd adjusted Bob's hours back to 25 to match the time clock, assuming the 55 was a typo. If it was an error, that was on Dick.

I was reviewing the day's schedules when the door opened. It wasn't Dick but Adrian Hightower, the Food and Beverage Director's second-in-command.

Adrian was a no-nonsense force who dressed in an endless rotation of high-end suits. He was the kind of leader I admired, someone who started as a dishwasher and fought his way to the top, never afraid to jump into the trenches with the staff. He was also the kind of man who would smile while tearing you apart for being disorganized.

I was surprised to see him because since I started here he had never once visited our office. Seeing him standing there now made me a bit nervous.

"What are you doing in here, AJ? Hiding out?" he asked.

"No," I said, my guard up. "I just finished the payroll, and—"

"Relax," he chuckled. "I know what you're doing. I always know what my managers are up to. I wanted to talk to you about a few things."

He spun a chair around, straddling it with a smile. "Good news or bad news first? Your choice."

"I'll take the good first."

"Ok. I came in early to see if you needed help with the payroll, but I see you've already finished it. Everything looked in order. You're proving I made the right call hiring you."

"Thank you", I said, a bit flushed. It was nice to be acknowledged for good work.

His expression turned serious. "It's important you succeed, AJ. There aren't many of us in management here. We're paving the way for those coming after us. You hear me?"

I nodded. "I understand."

Then he smiled his shark–like smile again. "Are you ready for the bad news?"

I took a deep breath and waited for the shoe to drop.

He continued, "Dick is dealing with a personal issue and he won't be coming in today, which means, you have to work a double shift. Will that be a problem for you?"

Shaking my head I replied, "No, I'm good with that. I didn't have any plans this evening anyway."

He nodded. "Good, occupancy is low, so you should be able to get out of here by eleven p.m. if all goes well. Just a heads-up, you may have to cover tomorrow as well, but I'll let you know for sure later this evening. I'll make up this last-minute schedule change to you with some extra PTO."

He began scanning the office, his eyes drifting over the desks, shelving and file cabinets. I found myself looking where he looked, wondering what he was searching for. Then his gaze snapped back to mine, his smile completely gone.

"AJ, let me give you some advice," he said. "When I interviewed you, I knew you lacked experience, but I saw that military fire in you. If you can manage Marines, you can manage anyone, but just like in the service, you have to learn the business—and you have to cover your ass at all times."

I was listening so intently that I didn't even flinch when my pager buzzed.

Adrian continued, "When you forgot to leave a detailed note in the manager's log about your discussion with Theresa at the Bistro Bar, and your interaction with Bob, you gave your boss, and his security boy, fuel to jack you up.

I couldn't believe my error. I was so focused on burying Bob in paperwork, I totally forgot to log the incidents in the logs book. Stupid me.

As he continued talking, he pulled something out of his inner pocket, "You also lost the only way to prove what isn't on this" and he tossed a VCR tape on my desk.

"I spoke with McGillicuddy," Adrian said. "He'll probably still say something to Dick, but I squashed that bullshit. I also talked to Theresa. She's a talker, so it wasn't hard to get the real story—you did right in reminded her what she should be doing and not doing."

He leaned in. "I saw Bob's write-ups, too. Dick won't be happy you put paper on his boy, but you two will have to settle that yourselves."

I didn't even realize my jaw had dropped. He really did know everything. Then he told me to get a notebook and record everything.

"Don't rely on memory. Write it down, then transfer it to the manager log after every shift. Over-document everything so nothing comes back to bite you—like that tape almost did."

I made a mental note to start doing that immediately.

"I know you work hard, AJ," he said. "Beverage is the toughest department to run, especially coming in cold with little or no hospitality background. I want you to see things from the perspective of our other associates over the next month. Are you open to that?"

"I'm definitely open to that," I replied, feeling a moment of gratitude for any opportunity to learn more about the industry.

"Great," he said. "I'll set up some trainings for you to begin next week. It'll help you support the team when things get heavy and make you a better-rounded manager. "Plus", he added with a knowing look, "it'll give you a break from Dick being in your ass at every turn."

He got up to leave, and before he exited the office, he turned toward me. "I'll email the details to you and Dick. Also, AJ, some of my managers are like crabs in a barrel. They will run over you so you don't advance or get noticed for your efforts just because the light isn't shining on them."

Before he exited the office he pointed at the VCR tape. "You have to figure out how to make your way to the top without being stepped on. And just for the record, I'm not going to save you again." And with those last words, he left.

Chapter 14

As the door clicked shut, I exhaled. Things were getting deep—maybe deeper than I'd signed up for. I grabbed the security tape, stomped it into shards, and tossed the wreckage into the trash.

The double shift went smoothly, and by eleven p.m., I was home. Adrian notified me that Dick was coming in the following day so I did not need to do another double. I was exhausted but energized by the prospect of training and the much-needed break from Dick.

Despite the hour, I decided to call Ronnie. She'd paged me earlier, but my talk with Adrian had completely wiped my mind. I rehearsed my opening, then dialed the number from the paper bag. It rang four times. I was ready to hang up when her voicemail kicked in: *"Hi, it's me. Sorry I missed your call. Leave a message and I'll try to link up with you soon... Bye."*

At the beep, I dropped my voice into the smoothest, sexiest tone I could muster.

"Hi Ronnie, its AJ. Just checking in on you. Give me a shout whenever you can. Hope to hear from you soon."

I wasn't ready for sleep, so I spent the next hour listening to music and flipping through *The City Paper*, half-expecting the phone to ring. It didn't.

I was back at my desk by ten the next day. When Dick finally rolled in at twelve-thirty, he barely acknowledged me. After a quick, muffled phone call, he barked an order to me without looking up.

"Go deliver a bottle of Veuve Clicquot to Housekeeping. And don't forget the transfer slip."

Shocked, I stood so abruptly that my chair legs scraped the floor. I stared him down. "Hey, man—start using your manners. I'm done with the disrespect. Do you understand me?"

Dick actually flinched and I saw the flash of fear in his eyes, but he masked it quickly. I grabbed the bottle from the cooler, and started on the required paperwork.

"Also," he added, his voice more authoritative now, "I talked to HR about Bob. Your write-up stands, but don't you ever discipline another associate without my approval again."

It was the opening I'd been waiting for. I sat down again, pulled out a small Moleskin notebook I had from my Marine days, and clicked my pen.

"So," I said, meeting his gaze. "What should I do if an associate violates policy on my shift while you're gone? Especially if you're unreachable?"

He was momentarily taken aback by the note-taking. "Just leave me the info. I'll handle it."

I scribbled that down. "Just so I'm clear: no matter what they do or what I suspect, I let them keep working and just report it to you? That applies to any circumstance, right?"

I looked up, pen poised. Dick was glowering now, his eyes actually locked on mine.

"Like I said, leave me the info or contact me before you do anything. Do you understand? Now, would you please deliver that champagne?"

Ignoring his much nicer request, I leaned across his desk, which bought on a look of uncomfortableness to his face.

"Dick, I called you for advice about Bob, but you didn't pick up, so I went by the HR manual.

I watched him bristle, but I didn't back down. "I will always try to reach you first but if I can't get you, I'm not just leaving a note. I'm going back to that manual and I'm going to discipline the associate according to what it says to do. So, in the future, I'm not letting someone stay on the clock who needs to be coached or sent home. Do you understand?"

Dick's usually pallid, veiny face turned a sudden, violent crimson. When he stayed silent, I pushed further.

"Also, did you read the email from Adrian about me starting cross-training in other departments next week?"

He looked away, scowling. "Yeah. I don't know how you expect to balance that with your shifts, but don't think I'm covering for you."

I made a show of scribbling in my Moleskin. I was actually just writing nonsense, but the sight of the pen moving clearly rattled him. I felt a surge of pride as I tucked the notebook back into my pocket and headed out with the champagne, leaving him stewing in his own confusion.

For the rest of the shift, Dick and I were ghosts to each other. I triple-checked every task and made sure to grin at every security camera I passed, knowing the "ex-cop" was likely watching the feed.

Later, Adrian emailed my training schedule. It was for five week and the catch? I still had to cover several evening shifts a week. It was going to be brutal, but I was as happy as a lark—and I'm sure Dick was thrilled to have me out of his hair.

Chapter 15

My first day of training landed me in the Stewarding Department with the scullery crew. The GM (General Manager) offered to let me shadow him and his managers, but I declined. I wanted the associate level experience, so I suited up in their uniform and dove in.

The work was grueling, but I loved it. The stewards reminded me of Marines: a rowdy band of misfits talking trash and joking through the grind. It opened my eyes to a hard truth—the people with the "lowliest" jobs were the engine of the hotel. If they ever decided to slow down, they could paralyze the entire operation.

By the end of the week, I was back in Beverage to cover the weekend. I was exhausted from the scullery, but I refused to let it show.

Friday evening hit with a "sold out" alert from the Front Desk. We had five part-time bar backs for full-house surges, but Dick had spitefully scheduled only one: Vidal, the veteran of the group. I tried calling the others for backup, but on such short notice, no one could make it. Dick was clearly punishing me for my time away.

When I broke the news to Vidal, he spat, "*Esa puta polla!*" My Spanglish was rough, but I didn't need a translator to know he was calling our boss exactly what he was—a fucking dick.

We hunkered down and split the workload. We got our asses kicked, but we survived. Before clocking out, I documented the scheduling sabotage in my Moleskin and made a note to get Vidal the recognition he deserved.

I spent Sunday afternoon sleeping off the weekend. Still no word from Ronnie, but I was too drained to care.

On Monday morning I traded my scullery rags for a suit and reported to the Concierge Department—which was really just a lone, unadorned podium. It was manned by a young guy named Micah (pronounced *Me-Shay*), who was eager to show me the ropes.

For three days, I spent my mornings with him before heading back to the office for closing duties. Whenever I was back in our warehouse-office, I started noticing a pattern: high-end empty liquor bottles started appearing again, only to vanish by the next day. I had no idea what Dick was pulling, but I was just grateful our only interaction was through post-it notes and emails. On Thursday evening, I met with the Executive Chef, Charles, regarding my time with his team the following weeks. I'd seen him around, but we'd never spoken. He asked about my time in the Marines and I confessed my lack of professional kitchen skills, but he shrugged and added me to the schedule anyway. Adrian had pre-approved a ten-day stint for me to help cover for his staff who were overdue for time off.

I was already dreading the thought of eight-hour kitchen shifts followed by six hours of management duties, but Chef Charles cut me a break.

"Just so you know," he said, "your boss isn't high on my list. I don't like him and I don't like how he runs his shop. I've cleared it with Adrian: while you're with me, you won't be responsible for bullshit doubles, but be ready, we've got some busy days coming up and I'm short-handed."

He handed me a pair of black utility pants and a chef's jacket with my name stenciled on the chest.

Chef didn't know it, but after his declaration, I would pretty much do anything to help him and his team. The next two weeks were going to be interesting.

The first week I worked in the Bistro kitchen, and it was a crash course in prep and the grill. I saw Miss Theresa almost daily—her stool was now a permanent fixture at the bar, and as usual, she debuted a new wig every shift.

Things were going smooth until I was assigned to grill some marinated chicken. That day I learned the hard lesson of why you don't overload a grill. I started a small grease fire that nearly took out a section of kitchen. After extinguishing it, I took a verbal lashing from the Sous Chef and was ordered to scrub the grill. As I scrubbed with a wire brush, I caught sight of Dick standing across the kitchen, sneering at me and my manual labor. I just kept scrubbing and ignored him.

The physical grind was so much that once I got home I was out the second my head hit the pillow.

The next week I moved to the Bakery under the Pastry Chef. After a quick tutorial, I was cut loose to prep fifteen loaves of sourdough. It was a different kind of labor—kneading dough until my forearms burned—but the air-conditioned bakery felt like a luxury after the heat of the other parts of the kitchen.

While the dough raised, I slipped out for a quick break and a smoke. Tucked just out of sight from the associate entrance, I spotted Bob leaving the hotel. He was moving with purpose, his backpack suspiciously bulging, was slung heavy over his shoulder. I noticed he was purposely walking in the blind spots of the exterior cameras. It looked practiced, like he had done that many times before.

A few minutes later, both Dick and McGillicuddy walked out. They didn't bother hiding from the lenses and they caught up with Bob out on Pratt Street. After a quick huddle, the three of them vanished around the corner.

I pulled out the Moleskin and scribbled: *11:45 a.m., March 23rd.*
Bob leaving the hotel with bulky backpack, dodging cameras. Met with Dick and Security Chief on Pratt St. The 3 of them are up to some shit!

Chapter 16

My final training week was in the Purchasing department, run by a guy named Abyasa who'd been there since the hotel opened in '82. This team managed the lifeblood of the property ordering everything that was needed to run the hotel successfully.

After a quick introduction, Abyasa skipped the small talk and gave me a "Food and Beverage Boot Camp," diagramming the entire supply chain on a whiteboard. It was a complete shift in vibe from the kitchen or the scullery.

Shortly afterwards, I was assigned the task of inventorying toilet paper. Abyasa handed me a clipboard and a calculator and sent me into the warehouse stacks. It took me ninety minutes to get a count of 3,414 rolls. Abyasa took one look at my number, shook his head, and sent me back to do it again, but slower. It took three attempts before he accepted a final count and it was still off by a few. Five hours of counting toilet paper would break anyone so he finally cut me loose for the day. All night long I couldn't get toilet paper out of my head.

The next morning, Abyasa explained that he was strict with his numbers because he had learned that accurate inventory was the foundation of everything—forecasting, cost control, and shrinkage.

"Inaccurate counting will kill any success you want to achieve," he warned. "It ultimately affects the hotel's bottom line, your job security, and your bonus." I realized then that I'd never seen Dick show even a fraction of this concern.

On my final day, Abyasa gave me the heads-up: Adrian had granted me the following day off, but I was slated for doubles Monday and Tuesday. Before letting me go early, he pulled me into his office for a smoke.

"AJ, you've done well, but watch you're back with Dick," he said gravely. "He has a history. The moment an assistant manager gets too good at the job, he finds a way to erase them."

He continued, "Also, you should learn everything you can about bartending. It is more than just mixing and making drinks. You'll never be a truly effective department leader if you can't do what your associates do and be able to jump in and support them. Plus, it'll help you identify over pouring and theft. Those two things will wreak havoc on your liquor cost.

He offered to be a resource if I needed anything, and I shook his hand, truly grateful. That was yet another person warning me that my boss would have it in for me as I got better at my job.

On the bus ride home, I flipped through my Moleskin. The last five weeks as a masterclass in hotel operations, and the relationships I'd built were priceless. I noticed one consistent theme: no one had a single good thing to say about Dick.

As I looked at my notes on the "ghost employee" hours and the three assholes suspicious meeting on Pratt Street, I realized I wasn't just a Trainee anymore—I was becoming an Investigator.

I hopped off the bus in Bolton Hill and hit the market. A month of fast food and employee cafeteria leftover-mish mash was enough. I stocked up on staples and, more importantly, beer. Outside, I used the payphone to page Ronnie one more time, crossing my fingers for a callback.

By 2:30 p.m., I was back at the apartment. With the neighbors out, I claimed the patio garden, cracked a brew, and lit a week-old joint to the sound of a jazz station. The high and the hops hit me fast. I stashed my half-finished beer, showered, and was out cold by 4:17 p.m.

I blinked awake at 11:15 p.m. to *Shakedown Dance Party* on Channel 13. Sitting there eating Verde salsa and tortilla chips, I laughed at a quote I'd read: *Bachelors are like summer breezes— never as cool as they pretend to be.*

Chapter 17

Sunday morning, I started my day off with an Irish coffee, spiked with my last shot of Old Crow. Then it hit me: I'd turned off my pager days ago. I scrambled to power it up, praying for a hit from Ronnie, but the screen stayed blank. Oh well.

The fact that today was also laundry day was a no brainer. I'd been out of clean underwear for forty-eight hours and my last towel was turning sour.

I bundled the mess, clipped my lock-blade to my belt, and headed across North Avenue to the laundromat. Even on a quiet Sunday, I wasn't ignoring those ladies warnings about the block.

After firing up the washers, I stepped next door to the liquor store to restock. After making my selections, I was now in the back of a checkout line that was at a standstill. There was a teenaged boy at the counter having an argument with the owners. He was trying to return a fifth of Crown Royal and was losing that battle.

"Just give me the cash, Papasan," the kid snapped. "My auntie bought it yesterday and changed her mind. She told me to get her money back. The seal ain't even broken!"

The male owner said, "You no buy here … you no have receipt, and I never see you … sorry."

Then to all of us in line, as if to prove they wouldn't dare violate any state law, the wife angrily said, "Him not even age to buy!"

The kid shouted back, "I tole you Chinks, I didn't buy it … my auntie did! There ain't nuthin wrong with it. She jus' want da money back!"

"We no Chinese!" the wife screamed, slamming her hand down. "We Korean, and we from Bawl'more!"

While the kid kept hollering about his "auntie" and the refund, the husband calmly picked up the Crown Royal. He was scrutinizing the bottle when—the cap unscrewed with a simple twist. He took one whiff, shook his head, and tossed the whole thing into the trash and said something to his wife in Korean.

After that, the wife went nuclear. She grabbed the phone, screaming at the kid that the seal was fake and the bottle was full of iced tea. "You leave now or I call Po-lice!"

Several of us in line laughed as the kid elicited curses while quickly moving to the door. On the way out he yelled over his shoulder, "Fuck you, Chinks!"

The shop owners were angry and animatedly talked back and forth in Korean about the potential rip-off. As I waited patiently to pay for my whiskey, I kept thinking that the kid's scheme seemed familiar, but I couldn't put my finger on how.

I spent the rest of my Sunday in low gear—folding laundry, prepping a sharp outfit for Monday's double, picking at leftovers while mentally preparing for the upcoming week. My final task for the day was to call Driver and arrange an early morning pick-up.

I was lying in bed when one of my upstairs housemates started singing along to Wilson Phillips new song "Hold On." She really liked that song, because she restarted it four more times. Her voice wasn't good, but she sang it with conviction. I fell asleep humming along to her off-key harmonizing.

I arrived at The Regency just before 9:15 a.m.—two hours early. Carrying my suit in a garment bag while dressed for labor in jeans and boots, I found exactly what I expected: Dick had done nothing to set us up for success. I wasn't even that angry; I was just pleased that I was learning how to beat him at his own game.

I was aware that the hotel was currently sold out and was hosting the annual North American Construction Executives meeting. Digging through the files, I found a detailed history from their last visit—which had obviously been written by a former assistant rather than in Dick's left-handed chicken scratch. Based on the report, these guys were heavy consumers who put away gobs of liquor, American beer, and red meat.

By the time the staff clocked in, I had every outlet stocked to the gills. It was a good thing, too—we were 'balls to the walls' busy until last call. Vidal and I did a good job schlepping and ensuring that every banquet hall and bar throughout the hotel was stocked continuously.

By 10:30p.m I was drained. In the back of my mind I was fully aware that tomorrow, I was pulling a *clopen*. It's a closing shift backed up by the next day's opening shift. This was the industry's special brand of hell!

At 2:15a.m., I stood at the hotel rear entrance waiting for Driver. I was barely upright. I crashed the second I hit the passenger seat and didn't wake up until we arrived at my apartment. Once inside, I took a shower, crawled into bed, and that was the last thing I remembered.

<u>**Chapter 18**</u>

The following morning I was grinding through labor reports and credit card batches. I don't normally drink coffee at work but I needed it today. I was about to take another much needed gulp when I noticed the two haphazardly closed alcohol boxes under Dick's desk. The boxes of alcohol were not suspicious, but the condition of the boxes peaked my curiosity. There were wet spots on the cardboard and there was a blue funnel next to them on the floor. I could not help it-I looked inside.

In the first box I found what looked like twelve full bottles of Grey Goose. The second held twelve empty Smirnoff bottles—all uncapped. What did Dick need empty Smirnoff bottles for? A quick inspection confirmed what I suspected: the Grey Goose bottles were full, but every single seal was broken.

It was then that I remembered the kid at my neighborhood liquor store. Was it possible that Dick was running his own version of the same scheme? Without having seen him do anything firsthand, I couldn't prove it, but I was certain that there was some fuckery going on.

Because I still had a shift to run, I couldn't focus any more of my time trying to figure out what exactly was going on, so I slid the boxes back under Dick's desk, logged the discovery in my Moleskin, and headed out to the floor.

By mid-morning the hotel's vibration shifted from chaotic to relax. After a busy recuperative brunch, the construction conventioneers had finally run out of steam and had begun checking out en masse.

As I made my rounds I noticed a change in the atmosphere. The staff members who had previously ignored me were suddenly chatty. The scuttlebutt was that Dick had loaned me out to the other departments as a punishment, but the real source of my new clout was simpler—I'd pulled off something unprecedented.

In the history of the hotel, no manager had ever cross-trained through the entire Food and

Beverage division, let alone by getting their hands dirty as a line-level employee. I had earned some major respect.

While checking on the banquet rooms, I was suddenly called to the Lobby bar to assist Daniela, a stunning server who bore a striking resemblance to Stacey Dash, with reprinting a sales receipt.

As I worked at the Point of Sales system, Daniella came up behind me startling me. She was so close I could feel her breasts pressed against my back. I played it cool as she looked over my shoulder and her breath was hot on my neck.

"You doing alright?" she asked in my ear.

"Yeah," I replied, hoping she couldn't see me blushing. "I think I've got it."

Quickly finishing up what I was doing, I handed her the reprinted receipt. She gave me a devious smile and said, "Thanks, AJ. Don't be such a stranger, or you'll make me think you don't like me."

I muttered a quick "Okay" and retreated before my smaller head could talk me into trouble.

The rest of the shift was quiet—a welcomed break from the previous forty-eight hours—but the boxes under Dick's desk acted like a magnet for my thoughts. Every time I went into the office I expected them to be gone, but every time, they were still there waiting, like a question-waiting for me to answer.

When I finished my reports, I realized that I couldn't leave it alone. I had to find a way to prove my theories.

Tossing around a few ideas I finally settled on one that just might work.

When I was finished I put the boxes and funnel exactly as I'd found them and left for the evening. I was smiling when I exited the building.

<u>**Chapter 19**</u>

The following morning my alarm woke me out of a dead sleep. I'd forgotten to clear it for my day off. All attempts to fall back asleep proved useless so I lay there listening to the girls moving around in the house above. I was also imagining what it would be like to finally wake up with a woman in my bed.

As an erection started to stir, I decided it was time to get out of the bed. I was fine being single, but the post-masturbation loneliness wasn't a vibe I wanted to start the day with.

Breakfast was a toasted bagel with sun-dried tomato cream cheese, mango juice, and a cup of Chai. I checked my pager and was surprised to find a note from Ronnie.

Mister AJ. It's Ronnie. I know we've been playing phone-tag, but things have been crazy with work. I'm off tomorrow so maybe we can get together if you got some time. Hit me ... Ronnie.

The timestamp showed she'd paged yesterday. I dialed her back immediately. No answer, so I left a message: I was off today and waiting on her call.

I had just turned on some morning jazz when the phone rang. I let it ring three times—because I didn't want to seem too eager for Ronnie. I answered in my smoothest baritone. "Hello?"

"Hi, good morning. I'm calling for Alicide Porter?" The voice was professional, female, and definitely not Ronnie.

"Speaking," I said, my tone now flat. "How can I help you?"

The caller said her name was Rachel Duke, and she was a talent scout for Hospitality Pro Search. She'd said she pulled my resume from a VA transition program. I'd forgotten I even signed up for that a year ago. She was chirpy and eager to talk about job opportunities, but I wasn't hearing it.

"I'm happy where I'm currently employed," I told her, shutting the door before she could even make her pitch at me.

But Rachel had the tenacity of a used car salesman. Just as I was about to hang up, she pivoted. "AJ, the industry is blowing up. I have local roles that would be a perfect fit—roles that would definitely increase your income, your happiness, and your wellbeing."

She hooked me with that last bit.

I turned down the jazz and we talked for an hour. She broke down the market, while I explained my current role. By the time she ran out of gas, I'd agreed to let her mail me an application and background forms, just in case.

No sooner had I hung up when the phone rang again. This time, the voice on the other end was smoky. "Hello there, AJ. This is Ronnie."

A huge smile broke across my face. "Well, hello there yourself. You're a hard lady to catch."

"Sorry," she said. "I got your pages, but like I said, I've been buried in double shifts. I finally have a day off, though. Want to get together?"

"Most definitely. What did you have in mind, and when?"

"How about right now?" she asked. "I'm dying to get out of the house. I can head out your way and we'll figure it out from there. I'll grab something to drink on the way, if it's not too early for you?"

"That's cool," I said, and gave her the address and directions to the patio-garden entrance.

"See you in twenty."

I showered, dressed, and changed my bed linens. I was still straightening the kitchen when the buzzer at the alley went off. I checked the convex mirror I'd mounted at the gate and saw Ronnie smiling back. She looked radiant in a yellow sundress that popped against her brown skin. She paired the dress with some lace-up gladiator sandals and had a beach bag on her shoulder.

I swung the gate open and greeted her, "That was fast. Come on in."

We spent the first half-hour just catching up, bridging the gap since we'd last spoken. As we talked, I found myself stealing glances at her, tracing the curves of her body beneath the thin fabric of the sundress.

"Nice place," she said, scanning the room. "Mind if I look around?"

"Go ahead, but you've pretty much seen all of it already when you came in"
She stopped at my bookshelf, trailing her fingers over the spines.

"You actually read all of these?"

"Oh yeah, some twice. It started in grade school—teachers used to kick me out of class and send me to the library as punishment. They didn't realize they were just giving me an escape from being bored to death."

"I try to read," she admitted, "but I usually just fall asleep."

She kept browsing before turning back to me when I asked her what the plan was for today.

"Honestly? If you'd tried to jump me the second I walked in, or if this place was a wreck, I would've suggested we go out—then made an excuse to leave, but your place is cool so can we just hang here?"

I smiled. "Works for me. Because of my own busy schedule, I've only been using this place to shower and sleep lately."

Then she exclaimed, "I almost forgot! I brought refreshments."
She reached into her beach bag and lined up two bottles of J. Roget champagne and a quart of OJ on the counter. She caught me beaming at her.

"Why you grinning like that?"

"Three things. One, it took forever, but I'm glad to finally see you in person. Two, I love mimosas, and three, you're my first guest and you showed up with gifts."

That earned me a matching grin. As I tucked the bottles into the fridge, she said, "I forgot to ask— do you smoke weed?"

"Jah give thanks," I laughed. "I most definitely partake in the sacrament."

She produced a Ziploc bag with bright green buds and three pre-rolled joints from her bag.

"Good, because I need to get lifted. I've got a couple of sticks ready. Why don't you mix those drinks?"

Chapter 20

The setup was simple: a boom box, a wooden table, and a stick of incense to catch the breeze. After a quick trip back inside for a leather footrest, Ronnie looked genuinely pleased as she settled her feet onto it. The day was off to a promising start.

I tuned the radio to *Magic 95.9*, and after a few commercials, Jodeci's "Come and Talk to Me" kicked in. We both nodded along, passing the spliff back and forth while sipping our drinks.

When the song faded out, Ronnie broke the silence. "Do your upstairs housemates ever come down here?"

"Not that I know of," I said. "I hardly ever see them."

She took a drag of the joint and passed it back.
"Do you even know who they are?"

"They're three girls from the Art Institute. That's
about the extent that I know. I briefly met them
when I moved in, but the only time I really know
they're home is when I hear them moving around
above me."
I refreshed our drinks, and as we were now high,
we switched to cigarettes.

Suddenly a bit serious she said, "Hey, I know you
called me a few times and I'm really sorry I didn't
get back to you sooner. My job is very demanding
and doesn't give me time for much else."

"Believe me, I understand." I told her about my
job and my weeks of training. "Seems like both of
us were super busy and needed a break."

When she told me she was getting the munchies, I
asked if she wanted us to go get something to eat.

With her voice tinged with weed, champagne, and
cigarette smoke, she said, "I'm right where I want
to be. Can we order some delivery instead?"

"There's a Chinese joint named Chang's across the street that's decent, and they even make pizza."

She laughed "Them Chinese cover all their bases and will try their hand at making whatever will sell. Let's see how they do pizza."

I went inside, dug the menu out of the junk drawer, and called. While I was on hold, Ronnie tapped my shoulder. She had lit another joint and with expert skill, she pulled until the cherry blazed red, flipped the lit end into her mouth, and motioned me close.

She blew me a shotgun, our lips meeting in a thick, smoke-filled kiss. Her hands caressed my face as she channeled a steady stream of smoke into my lungs. By the time she pulled away, I was brick-hard. She just laughed while I coughed my way through an order for a pepperoni pizza.

After I hung up, she was back at the bookcase, this time scanning my CDs. She turned with a playful look. "So, you've read some of these more than once, huh? Does that mean when you like something, you keep coming back to it? I hope I can be one of your favorites, too."

"You're already getting to be my favorite."

We talked some more and our conversation drifted into why neither of us was currently in a relationship, and why we were enjoying being single. I told her that I'd been married for two years and wasn't looking for a repeat performance and she seemed to be on the same page.

Stepping closer, she tilted her face up to mine. Our mouths met, and she wrapped her arms around my waist, pulling me in until the heat between us was undeniable. I knew she could feel my hard-on pressing against her.

She broke the kiss, breathless. "If we don't stop now, they'll sell our pizza to someone else. You better pick it up before we go too far."

I grabbed my wallet. "Be right back."

Before heading back I made a quick stop at the liquor store, grabbing a six-pack of Red Stripe, a pint of Blackberry Brandy, and a three-pack of condoms.

Chapter 21

Re-entering the patio garden, I heard the sound of Sade's _Is It a Crime_ on the air. Inside the apartment Ronnie was crooning along to it and I noticed that she'd made herself at home. She had swapped out the sundress for frayed denim shorts that left little to the imagination, and had on one of my Marine Corps tank tops. She'd clearly been snooping through my house.

On any other day, I would've been pissed, but I'd already made sure my cash, documents, and weapons were well-hidden before she ever buzzed the gate.

The tank top was too big for her even though she'd tied it off at her waist. She didn't have on a bra either so I knew I was getting laid tonight.

I set the items on the counter as the smooth R&B of Tony! Toni! Toné! filled the room. Ronnie sashayed into the kitchen, humming along to *"It Never Rains in Southern California"* and perched expectantly at the breakfast bar.

"Hope you don't mind," she said, "but I borrowed a shirt."

"No problem at all," I replied, catching a glimpse of side-boob as she reached for a slice. I poured us some shots and cracked two Red Stripes. The pizza was actually decent—Chang's had pulled it off.

Between bites, Ronnie's expression suddenly shifted.

"AJ, I haven't been completely honest."

I froze, praying whatever was coming wouldn't kill the mood.

"Yeah? About what?"

She took a small bite of pizza, chewing slowly while I waited for her next words. Looking a little embarrassed, she said.

"Remember Carrie, the girl you met me with at the bar? Well, she's not just my coworker and roommate. She's also my lover too."

I poured us both healthy shots of brandy--to help cushion the blow of her words, as well as numb the sting of seeing my hopes of getting laid dashing away. She went on to explain that she met Carrie while they were both at nursing school and they became fast friends.
"She was fun to hang out with, and we both got lucky and landed jobs at the VA Hospital after graduation. As we were both just starting our careers, sharing an apartment just seemed like a smart financial move at the time."

I agreed and took a bite of pizza.

"Back then, the thought of being with a woman hadn't even crossed my mind. I'd seen lesbian porn, sure, and felt a flicker of interest, but I was strictly into men. She probably had designs on me from the start; I just missed the signs. Anyway, I started noticing things—like the way she started flirting with me at home, but I'd just brush it off. Then, one Friday last winter, everything changed."

I nodded, silently wondering why she was dropping something this heavy on me, especially since we barely knew each other. Could it be a test or was it something so personal she could only tell a stranger, or was she just really high?

In between bites and sips, Ronnie told me about how last winter after they worked a brutal ten-hour shift they were going to have some drinks at home. Eventually, Carrie convinced her to hit a lesbian-warehouse party off the Harbor called Heaven's Gate.
"On the way there we shared a joint with the cabbie. The place was packed. House music was pumping, and it was like a furnace in there despite the cold outside. We found a corner to people-watch, and that's when I realized Carrie was pressed against my back, her arm snaked around my waist. And you know what, AJ? I didn't push her away. I was high, and the attention felt good."

She grinned, caught in the memory. "After a little bit I figured if we got on the dance floor it would help clear my head. Plus, it would put some space in between us. That DJ was killing it! Even the dead would've had to move to that beat."

Her voice dropped an octave. "Then the music switched to a slow groove. Next thing I know, Carrie's kissing my neck *exactly* how I like it, and I just...went with it. Everyone was locked together, kissing and grinding. The air was thick with sensuality and I got swept up in the erotic atmosphere.”

An internal war was breaking out in my body. My brain was flagging her as unstable and to get away, but my dick was over-ruling the motion, insisting we see where this was going. I got us fresh beers, she lit a joint and dove back into her story.
 “When we left the floor, I was parched, and wanted water. Carrie went for the drinks while I hit the bathroom line. Instead of water, she came back with a cocktail. I didn't want it, but she started talking shit about how after paying for it and me wasting her money. She talked me into chugging the whole thing.” Her expression clouded. “That’s the last thing I remember clearly. Everything went foggy.”

“Foggy?” I leaned in. “Like you blacked out?”

“Not passed out, just... bits and pieces are foggy. It could have been a mix of things, but I think she might have roofied me.”

The confidence she’d been showing vanished, replaced by visible embarrassment. She shook her head as if trying to physically clear the memory.

"Next thing I know," she continued, "We're both naked in my bed. Carrie has her face buried between my legs, and I'm having an orgasm. Look, I like Carrie, but I'm still into men. Basically what I'm trying to say is that, I'm bisexual."

Hope was alive again with that confession, and my dick began twitching. Ronnie took a breath and continued.
"Since that first night, we've slept together a few times, but now she wants a relationship. We got into it last night because she called me a tease—said I walk around the apartment half-naked and then turn her down. I told her it's my body and I decide when and who I share it with. If she doesn't stop sweating me, I'm moving out. I like being single. I like being free."

She fell silent, locking eyes with me. A new fear hit: was she about to ask to move in? I definitely wanted to get laid, but I wasn't sure I was willing to pay *that* high a price. I emptied the ashtray, careful to save the joint.

"Damn," I said, settling back. "You've got yourself into some real shit. Unrequited love is a hard pill to swallow, man or woman. You can't keep living in that atmosphere—it's only a matter of time before things get dangerous."

Ronnie blew a plume of smoke and raised her glass. We toasted in silence as Lenny Kravitz's *"It Ain't Over, 'til it's Over"* filled the room. Then we both sat listening to the music; as if she had purged herself of some great telling and I was analyzing what the real reason was she chose me as her confessor.

Chapter 22

When our silence became uncomfortable I looked up to find her wearing that same sexy smile from earlier. She signaled me with her hand, forming a gun with her index finger before slowly tilting it downward.

I followed the point. My eyes dropped to the countertop, then shifted to the oversized Marine Corps tank top. My tank-top had drifted, and I was staring at her fully exposed breast. I think all the talk about sex with Carrie had turned her on.

She was pointing at the joint in the ashtray, but she meant for me to see her breast. When I looked back up, she had that mischievous, canary-eating grin.

"See something you want?" she asked, her voice dropping back into that smoky register. "You just gonna let it sit there, or are you gonna do something about it?"

I didn't need to be told twice. I reached for the joint, caught her eye, and smiled. I relit the herb, blew off the ash, and rounded the breakfast bar. She stood to meet me and I leaned in and blew her a shotgun, the smoke a bridge between us. When I finished, she took the joint, blew off ash, pulled deep, and returned the favor, her lips lingering on mine as she exhaled.

Between hits of smoke, we lost ourselves in a kiss. Her nails raked across my chest as she snaked a hand under my shirt. I pulled it over my head and dropped it; she answered by letting her denim shorts hit the floor. Not wanting to be left out, I kicked off my jeans and helped her out of the tank top. We didn't make it much further than the bedroom.

The next two hours were a blur. We started slow—gentle, sensual, romantic—before a gear shifted into something raw and lascivious; then it was no-holds-barred. We fucked like we were checking off every tucked-away fantasy on a list, leaving no inch of skin untouched, licked, or stroked. She wanted it rough, she wanted it loud, and I obliged. We disappeared into an erotic bubble of growls and sighs. The world was fantastic.

When we finally collapsed, gasping for air, Ronnie kissed my cheek. "AJ, I hate to do it, but I've gotta get moving. I have a pickup at the dry cleaners before they close. Mind if I use your shower?" I led her to the bathroom and handed her a fresh towel. She pinned up her locks and adjusted the spray. When she stepped in and held the curtain open with a look, I followed her in. We went at it one more time under the streaming water.

When she turned the water cold and started soaping up, I got the message and stepped out, leaving her to finish.

I was out in the patio garden when Ronnie emerged, fully dressed and beach bag in hand, looking exactly as she had when she arrived. She settled onto my lap with a smile.

"I had a great time today, AJ. You really know how to treat a girl. I hope we get the chance to do this again."

I searched her face, wondering if there was a hidden message in the invitation or if the "Carrie drama" was already calling her back. "I hope so, too," was all I said.

With hardly any fanfare, we walked out to her car. We shared a brief kiss through the driver's side window before she backed out and disappeared around the corner.

The goodbye felt woefully inadequate compared to the carnality we'd just shared, but I figured she had to *change up* before heading home to her girlfriend. I got a feeling that I would not see her again soon.

When I stepped back into the garden, one of my upstairs housemates was sitting in her windowsill, smoking. We exchanged a silent wave, and I couldn't help but wonder if she'd been listening to the porn movie Ronnie and I had just been making.

I straightened the patio, locked down the apartment, and collapsed onto the bed. I didn't even change the sheets. I fell into a deep sleep surrounded by the lingering scent of sex and Ronnie's hair on my pillows.

Chapter 23

The next morning, I was up early, nursing a coffee and still buzzing from yesterday. I wasn't due in until noon, but since starting early was paying off, I stuck with the routine. I called Driver; he picked up on the second ring and said he'd be there in twenty-five. By the time he pulled up, I was showered, dressed, and waiting out front. I went through the associate entrance turnstile at 9:35 a.m., silently hoping for a stress-free shift.

Outside the office, I heard the rhythmic *click-clack* of Dick's typing. Then another voice drifted through the door: "...they gon' have to pay up front this time... I ain't movin' on dat shit!"

When I entered the office, Dick quickly glanced at the clock, unprepared to see me this early, then he mumbled something quietly to his guest. The guy in my chair had his feet on my desk and a copy of the *Baltimore Sun* over his face, but those scuffed Doc Martens gave him away. It was Bob.

I offered a fake friendly "Good morning" and walked over to my desk. Neither the boots nor the paper budged. I knew that Bob knew I was there, so I said, "Bob, I need my desk."

He continued to ignore me, folding the paper to a new page with an exaggerated flourish and made a show of scanning the print, but we all knew he couldn't read.

I looked over at Dick, who was suddenly fascinated by something on his monitor. I could feel my peaceful morning vibe evaporating.

A scene of me turning over the entire desk and knocking Bob out of my chair flashed across my mind, but I pushed it away. I couldn't believe this was the same man who'd been sitting here a few days ago, snotting and crying. *This* Bob was putting on a performance, but he was about to learn that showmanship has its costs.

In a calm, but harder voice I said, "Bob, please get up from my desk. I'm not going to ask you again."

I expected Dick to de-escalate the situation at this point but he kept his head down and continued beating on his keyboard.

I had had enough. I took off my suit jacket, hung it on the coat rack, and then went back to my desk and stood directly over Bob-and just stared at him. I could tell he realized how volatile the moment had become because he was now trying to watch me without moving his head. I, in turn, was calculating how much violence it would take to dispatch him without him requiring serious medical attention.

When he couldn't handle it anymore, Bob snapped the paper shut and pulled his feet from on top of the desk. With an exasperated sigh, he threw the newspaper to the side, slammed his palm down on the desktop, and jumped up. My chair rolled backward and fell over. When he turned back to me, he was surprised to see I had not moved an inch. I stared, unblinking, into his face. Whatever he saw in my visage caused his blustering to fade.

Due to the configuration of the office, there was only one clear way for him to get from behind the desk, and I was blocking it.

In a small voice he said, "Ya gon' move so I can get past?"

He wanted that request to sound tough, but he sounded more pleadingly than he realized. When I didn't move he turned to Dick, who was now watching us.

"Dick, let me get behind you, before I fuck up this—

Before he could finish what he was saying, Dick scooted his chair up, jamming his stomach against his desk, and allowed Bob to side-scoot out against the wall. I never took my eyes off him.

When he got to the open area, he grinned back at me and said, "Thanks for letting me have the day off, boss. I'll talk to you later."

Bob then went over to a wooden pallet to retrieve his backpack, the same dingy-looking bag I'd seen him carrying in and out of the hotel. This morning, it was so heavy that it took him a little effort to heft it up onto his shoulder.

He strutted toward the office doors. Reaching out with his left hand, he pushed down the door handle while looking over his shoulder to mean mug me. Then, with extra bluster, he threw his left shoulder into the door to push it open.

When his shoulder hit the steel door he bounced back like a rubber ball because our office door swung in, not out. I almost laughed out loud, but at that exact moment, something in his backpack 'clinked', and I knew that sound—it was the sound of bottles knocking together.

Embarrassed at his stupidity, he tried look tough but I also saw a look of fear cross his face. He pulled open the door and quickly exited. Before I could go after him to investigate what was inside the bag, Dick was already up, around his desk and at the door. It was the quickest I'd ever seen him move. Over his shoulder he mumbled, "I'll take care of this" and was out of the office before I could object.

<u>*Chapter 24*</u>

I was glad I was alone in the office now because I was shaking from what had happened. I got my smokes from my inside jacket pocket and lit a cigarette. I puffed and paced around the office to calm down, pissed at Dick for not intervening with the situation with Bob. I was sure that there was stolen hotel liquor inside Bob's backpack, and I was disappointed at myself for not having done more to prove it.

I envisioned what would have happened if I had screamed my jarhead war cry, knocked Bob backward out of my chair, and turned the desk over on top of him. Even if they had both jumped on me, I had no doubt that even with their three arms and four legs, I would have seriously hurt them both. Things were getting bad and I had to do something about it.

I stubbed out my cigarette, up righted my chair, and sat down. I turned on my computer and as it powered to life with the usual series of beeps, clicks, whirs, and squeals, I brushed off the debris left from Bob's boots from the top of my desktop, got out my moleskin and started writing.

The office phone rang and interrupted my chronicling. I didn't have to start my schedule for at least another hour but I answered it anyway. I thought Dick would have been back by now, but he'd been gone for almost forty minutes.

In as calm a voice as I could muster, I answered, "Beverage department, this is AJ."

An anxious-sounding female voice said, "AJ, this is Michelle up in Poe's. Can I speak to Dick?"

Michelle was the GM of Poe's fine dining restaurant.

"He had to step out. Can I help you?"

"We have a VIP tasting for a wedding party in less than an hour, 20 people, and I don't have a body behind my bar! Do you know if he got a replacement for Faizon? He told me he'd call me back and let me know, but I haven't heard from him and I need a bartender."

I said, "Hold one moment, Michelle" and scanned Dick's desktop to see if he made a note, but there was nothing.

"Michelle, give me a few minutes and I'll have somebody up there to you. If not, I'll come bartend myself."

"Thanks AJ. Look, it's almost time for service and I got my staff started on the bar prep, mostly ice and fruit, but we need a bartender so please do something." She had to finish getting ready for service so she hung up.

It was now up to me to figure out something and quick. I decided that if I could get one of the back-up bartenders to come in, until that person arrived I could at least fill in and get the tasting started.

Taking Dick's rolodex off his desk, I flipped through it for the contacts. I tried three of the numbers and got no answer.

The only other option would be to shuffle around the staff I had on duty. I reviewed our staffing schedule to see who we had tonight. I had Amber at the Pool Bar, Alex at the Lobby Bar, a missing Faizon at Poe's, and Ms. Theresa at the Bistro Bar.

Amber was not really a bartender as she only pulled drinks from of a frozen drink machine. There was no way in hell, I would put Ms. Theresa in such an up-front position like the Lobby Bar, so that left Alex.

He was an experienced and dependable associate and he'd worked up in Poe's before. Knowing that he would make more money up there, he'd most likely be open to the switch.

I shrugged into my jacket, grabbed one of the stupid walkie-talkies, turned off the lights and exited the office.

I entered the men's locker room, grabbed a black service apron and wine opener from my locker, and headed to the Lobby.

After explaining the situation to Alex, I thanked him for being flexible, and sent him to report to Michelle.

Taking off my suit jacket, I neatly rolled up my sleeves and tied on a black service apron. Even with my limited experience, I could handle the Lobby Bar.

Chapter 25

The two cocktail servers on duty were Daniela and Amarath. Daniela was looking as sexy and pretty as usual, and flirting at me with her eyes whenever I looked at her. Dick had a crush on her, so he allowed her to work as much as she wanted. I wondered what she would think if she knew he had her in his secret file cabinet as "the beauty on duty with the booty."

Amarath was a short, pretty, olive-skinned woman. She was Vietnamese and French with waist-length jet-black hair, and had the build of a gymnast. She was a hard worker, but she was in Dick's shit file so he only scheduled her if he had no other choice. I was sure the only real reason he was had it out for her, was because she most likely didn't acquiesce to his come on.

When Alex left and I moved behind the bar I saw that he had already expertly set it up, so there wasn't anything to do but get acclimated to my new workstation. I was sure the ladies were wondering what I was doing there with an apron on.

Daniela was lighting candles and placing them along the bar top, while Amarath was placing an order at the service station.

Daniela asked me, "What you doing, AJ?"

I smiled and said, "Getting ready for service."

"Yeah, but you're a manager. Why are you here?"

Before I could answer, Amarath's ticket scrolled out of the service bar printer.

The order was for a Grey Goose Dirty Martini, a Maker's Mark Old Fashioned, and a glass of Stag's Leap Merlot. Acting like I wasn't nervous, I got to work on the order as the servers watched my every move.

I got a martini glass and examined it for cleanliness. I then filled it with ice and soda water from the gun, then pulled the bottle of Goose from the shelf. Before pouring from it, I checked the bottom of the bottle and sure as shit, there was the mark I'd placed on the suspect bottles.

Instead of using that bottle, I put it aside and grabbed the unopened display bottle. After pouring some into a pint glass of ice, I got a plastic bottle of olive brine out of the cooler and squirted some on top of the vodka and let it marinate. I put a mixing tin on the brine and pint glass, and gave it a couple vigorous shakes. I threw out the soda and ice and strained the mixture into the martini glass. I garnished it with a skewer of three green Sevillano olives.

Next, I grabbed a rocks glass, shook in a couple splashes of Angostura bitters, added about a teaspoon of natural sugar, and muddled the mixture. Then, I placed an ice ball in the rocks glass, poured in a four-and-a-half count of Maker's Mark and a splash of water, stirred the contents with a mixing spoon, and added a couple Luxardo cherries and a piece of orange rind. I wiped out a wine glass with a towel and poured in five and one-fourths ounces of Stag's Leap Merlot. I placed all three drinks onto Amarath's tray. Daniela smiled and nodded her approval.

A couple times during our night, the ladies had to coach me on how to create one of our signature cocktails, but for the most part, the shift went along nice and easy. They even began to include me in their conversation, and Daniela was being touchy-feely flirtatious with me every chance she could. It was hard for me to ignore her, but I powered through.

We were having a nice time when the inevitable happened: a crowd showed up and the Lobby Bar morphed into a party. We were slammed for about two hours, and I was so busy that I didn't have time to reflect on the drama that had transpired earlier in the office. All I could do was focus on trying my best to keep up with the orders coming out of the printer and taking care of my own guests seated at the bar. Then, as fast as it started, it fizzled out and died.

As we were recovering from the rush, all of a sudden, the ladies went silent. Their conversation stopped so abruptly that I looked around to see why. Dick was outside the Lobby seating area, glowering at me and cradling his right arm. I didn't know how long he had been standing there, but I secretly hoped he wouldn't come over. I just ignored him and went back to what I was doing.

I knew he was no longer standing there when they began talking again. I'd probably catch some blowback later for my staffing shuffle, and for me bartending instead of handling my managerial duties, but I didn't care. I felt I'd made the best decision, with the staff I had on duty.

Our last guests left at nine p.m. and the bar turned into a graveyard. I gave us all a break and closed the bar early instead of waiting until ten. I had made seventy-two dollars in credit card tips and twenty-nine dollars in cash. I transferred the charge tips to the servers equally and gave the cash to our bar back, Vidal. After saying good night and thanking them for helping me, I left and began my closing routine.

When I returned to the office to enter my manager's reports, the lights were on. Dick's desktop had been cleaned and organized, and as usual, he was gone.

Sitting alone in the office typing out my End of Day report, I decided not to include the incident with Bob, but I made sure to include my re-organizing the schedule and why I chose to work a line position.

I also made notes about my findings at the bar in my Moleskin.

Chapter 26

I was on the street by 10:15 p.m. and decided to walk home. I had half a joint stashed in my cigarette pack, an easy opening lock-blade knife in my pocket, and the innate ability to run like hell if things got sideways. I figured the thirty-five-minute walk would give me time to map out a move against Dick

The streets were thin, so the trek felt safe enough, but I still kept my head on a swivel. Even with the weed taking the edge off, I knew that even in Charm City, anything can happen to anyone, anytime.

I'd been so deep in my head that I'd drifted off-course, winding up in Bolton Hill via a route I didn't recognize. I stopped on Dolphin Street to light another smoke and get my bearings when a neon sign caught my eye: _The Royal Dolphin Street Tavern._

It looked like a bar someone had dropped right into the middle of a residential block. Before the thought even finished, I was already halfway up the steps and pulling at the door.

The place was a dive, and was a row house that had been hollowed out into one long room. Inside, a small crowd was scattered at deuces and along the bar. I grabbed a seat at the stick and was greeted by the bartender who took my order.

The bar top was a mess of gouges and marks, but it had been sealed to a high shine. The walls were a collage of vintage signs, graffiti stickers, and faded news clips, some artist was painting a mural of the Sistine Chapel on the ceiling. The crowd ran the neighborhood gamut, and the CD changer pumped out a solid mix of soul and rock, from old school dusty to current hits.

The bartender returned with a healthy shot of Old Crow, a pint of Natty Boh, and an ice water—all for a whopping $7.25. I liked this place already.

The shot went down with a burning ease, and before I could look up to order another, the barmaid was back with the Crow bottle.

"Rough day, hun?"

"You got that right."

She poured another hit then offered her hand and said, "Looks like your first time in here. I'm Stacey."

We shook and I said, "Yeah, first time. I'm AJ. I live around the corner. I was walking home and saw the sign."

Stacey gave me a smile. "Well, welcome. Watch it though. I did just like you. I wandered in here sixteen years ago and have been stuck here ever since. I got your first shot. Let me know if you need anything else." Then she went off to serve her other guests. This place kept gaining points.

Sitting there replaying the last couple of hours, I was proud of how I had handled the schedule predicament and I knew that I put our best ace in the most suitable position, based on the concept of ensuring our guests were taken care of by our most capable associates. I also knew that no matter how I handled the situation, Dick would have something negative to say to me, even though it was his fault.

I ordered a final shot with Stacey and asked her to close me out. Downing the liquor, I chased it with my beer and took a sip of water to wash it down. I paid, left her a fat tip, and headed for home.

On the rest of my walk home, I thought about the bottles I had marked. I now knew that my boss was doing something illegal. His anal behavior about keeping empty bottles, the invoices that didn't match our inventory, spilled liquor, funnels on the office floor, bottles with broken cap seals, and sneaky meetings out on the street. I just needed to put the pieces together to form a solid case.
Inside my apartment, I grabbed a notebook and pen. Between drags of a cigarette I started mapping out my suspicions.

Was Dick swapping well-liquor into top-shelf bottles and charging premium prices? If so, the hustle was ingenious—and dirty. His only blunders had been sloppiness and bringing in a liability like his cousin Bob and the Security chief. I wonder who else was in on it and how long had this been going on?

Looking back at the turnover of assistant managers in our department, the pattern became clear. Whenever someone caught a whiff of the scheme, Dick sabotaged them. Now, it was my turn. The more I wrote, the more the anger took hold. If I wanted to survive this, I couldn't just wait—I had to report what I'd found out.

Chapter 27

I didn't get much sleep that night and woke up still developing my plan. Our Food and Beverage Director, Pierre, got into the hotel around 9:30a.m. and Dick was scheduled in at noon. I wasn't scheduled to report to work until 4:00p.m., but I needed to get into the hotel before Dick so I could request a meeting with the Director and possibly someone from HR.

I decided I would lead with yesterday's incident involving Bob. While it wouldn't paint me in the best light, I need to get ahead of the narrative. I'll make it clear that the situation escalated only because of Bob's rude behavior and Dick's lack of support. I'll admit I was angry, but I'll be sure to sell that no physical assault took place.

I was also going to tell them about Dick's constant disrespect. If they didn't believe it, I was ready to demand a transfer.

Getting ready, I practiced presenting my evidence and suspicions regarding Bob's criminal activity and I just hoped the 'untouchable' hotel lore wouldn't hold up this time.

I was a little nervous about the meeting. Although I've interacted with Adrian, I never had reason to engage with his boss, Pierre.

Driver arrived at 9:00a.m. We rode listening to Junior Murvin's song "Police and Thieves" while I flipped through my Moleskine. At the Regency, I tipped him and hopped out. "Have a good day, yo!" he called after me. "And watch your ass with them folks!"

At this time of the morning, there may not have been a lot going on in the guest areas, but the back of house was a beehive of activity. I carefully made my way to our administrative offices located behind the front desk. It was too early for the secretary to be at her desk, so I walked up to the director's office door and was about to knock when it opened.

Standing in the doorframe, was Dick.

We were both shocked. What was he doing here? I glanced over his shoulder and could see the heads of Adrian and Pierre and they too looked surprised to see me. Dick lowered his head and mumbled something to the carpet and inched past me. I stood there trying to make some sense of what was happening. This was not even close to how I thought this morning would go.

With a half-smile, and a French accent, Pierre said, "Good morning, AJ. *Si vous plait, entre.* Ve were just discussing you. Have a seat and we'll be with you in a moment."

He pointed to the chair, and I stepped across the plush carpet, my nerves firing. Adrian gave me a barely perceptible nod as Pierre dialed a number. "Bonjour," Pierre said into the receiver. "AJ is here in the office. *Non, non,* he showed up on his own."

He hung up and looked at me. "It will be just a minute, then we can talk."

I'd come here to surprise them, but the tide had turned. Now, I just sat there, bewildered.

Chapter 28

There was an uncomfortable silence in the office as Adrian stared at his computer screen and typed on his keyboard. Pierre asked me if I would like something to drink, but I declined, and then there was a knock on the office door. The door opened and Rosemary, the Director of Human Resources, stepped inside.

She was someone that had a naturally bubbly disposition. I'd seen her around the hotel a few times and had even attended some training sessions that she conducted. This morning she was carrying a manila folder, and she was definitely not bubbly.

Before Rosemary fully entered the office, she turned and said to someone outside, "Please wait here. We'll call you if we need your assistance, thank you." As the door closed, I got a brief glimpse of the sour-faced Security Chief.

The energy in the office made the hairs on the back of my neck stand up. Something was

seriously going to go wrong, and I had an idea what it was. Sweat rolled down my side to the beltline of my suit pants.
Rosemary moved past me to a chair behind Pierre's desk without any greeting.

Pierre leaned back. "Rosemary, we haven't started yet, so you've missed nothing." Then he said in French: "*AJ, Prende place. Droit au but, nous avons reçu une plainte.*"

When I gave him a blank look, he caught himself.

"I'm sorry, I switch without thinking. Take a seat AJ. Straight to the point, I received a complaint about you from the company's Ethics Hotline. Can you explain what happened yesterday between you and Bob Wilcott?"

Shit. Dick had beat me to the punch.

Suddenly, the office seemed smaller. I kept fighting to keep confidence on my face and act like what Pierre said hadn't fazed me.

I said to them, "If you don't mind, I'd like to stand." If HR was here, with security outside the office, this was my swan song.

I stood and cleared my throat, then began, "Bob and I did have an interaction yesterday in our office and that's part of why I came in early this morning, to talk to you all about it. I don't know what the complaint is, but it was hardly serious enough to be called into someone."

Rosemary chimed in. "I would disagree with that AJ; but why don't you humor us with the details of what you believe was not that serious."

I explained to them exactly what happened in the office and when I was finished, the room was silent and they were all looking at me.

Pierre said, "So to be clear, according to your version of *l'incedent*, at no point did you touch Bob or tell him you would kick his ass?"

"Not at all!" I answered.

Rosemary cut in, "But you *did* imply you'd get physical if he didn't move?"

Before I could get a word out, she opened the folder with a bit of theatrical flair and pulled a single sheet of paper.

"I have the transcript from his call. This is Bob's statement: '*I felt threatened and afraid for my physical safety. I was intimidated. I felt that if I didn't get up, I would be assaulted by my manager, AJ.*' "

Blood rushed to my ears and I wanted to shout, "That's bullshit!" Instead, I forced out a slow breath.

"Look," I said, as calmly as I could muster. "I didn't imply a thing. I told you exactly what I said. If Bob inferred something else, it's because he knew he'd crossed a line and was waiting for the blowback. He was probably just as shocked that Dick didn't jump in to save him."

I took a slight step forward. "And let's be real—if you've ever actually spoken to Bob, you know he doesn't use words like *intimidated* or *assaulted*. His cousin, coached him on every syllable and word of that statement."

I looked to Adrian for some sort of guidance, but he was back to studying something on his computer screen.

Rosemary spoke up and sternly said, "AJ, thanks for explaining, but whenever a call is logged to that line, it not only goes to the Executive Leadership at that property, it also goes to our corporate legal team, and they inform our owners. At the Grand Regency International Hotel & Suites, we take pride in our responsibilities and efforts to support our associates and investigate any complaints. If we didn't investigate and follow up each case properly, we could be liable for potential lawsuits and unwanted media attention. In this instance, your department manager, Dick, also witnessed what happened whit the associate and confirmed what he said on the ethics call."

Chapter 29

A sudden laugh escaped from me before I could even realize it. The sound startled the room and even caught me off guard. I got control of myself and saw that no one else was amused. When I reached inside my jacket pocket to pull out my Moleskin, I could see concern come across all their faces. I'm sure they were glad to see it was only a notebook.

I was still smirking when Rosemary said, "I fail to see the humor in this situation, AJ."

"Rosemary, I understand what happens when an ethics complaint has been made. In fact, I've contemplated lodging my own for harassment, disrespect, and possible racial prejudice against Dick for months now; but instead of whining to someone on the ethics hotline, I kept my head down and worked hard. After what happened yesterday, I got to the end of my rope and decided I would come and talk to you all first but, that doesn't matter much now." I saw the confusion on all three of their faces.

"And just so you know, I laughed because it's ironic and funny that you don't see this for what it is. I'm the fourth Assistant in our department in what—two years? How is there a revolving door of Assistants in one department while the Manager is the only constant? Does that not seem strange to any of you?

When no one said anything I continued.

"Dick's a lazy, abusive bully who stays comfortable because he thinks he's untouchable. He's confident that no matter the offence, it'll be fixed or overlooked. Dick is very much aware that he has you all over a barrel and that he'll never be fired."

Looking down, I opened my Moleskin and said, "Although this probably won't make a difference, I'd like to share some of the things that happened to me while working under Dick. It might help you see that things are not right in your Beverage Department."

I began rattling off a ledger of dates and times, citing every instance of disrespect and unfairness I received from Dick. I laid out the pattern of malicious, backstabbing behavior, recounting story after story.

Then I recounted the evening I caught Bob drinking on the job at a Bar Mitzvah and mentioned finding Dick's private stash of HR files tucked away in the back of his desk drawer when I was looking for the HR Manual. I explained how I discovered in those files that Bob was not only Dick's first cousin, but that his file was buried under a stack of disciplinary records that Dick had never officially filed with HR.

I also revealed the existence of a 'phantom employee', a person I'd never once seen in our department, and whose handwritten hours I was sure was being funneled directly to Bob.

Pierre was now furiously scribbling notes on a piece of paper, Adrian was leaning back in his chair with his fingers laced together behind his head, grinning broadly, and Rosemary, she looked like she no longer wanted to be in that room. She also looked like she hated me, but I was beginning to feel better. Then, I dropped my bombshell.

I voiced my suspicion that Dick was swapping top-shelf liquor for cheap brands at our bars and catering events.

I flipped to the pages I had dog-eared and detailed my findings regarding the empty bottles, spilled liquor, and stained boxes. I even pointed out the funnels that looked as though someone had simply forgotten to hide them.

I revealed the trap I'd set. How I had marked the bottom of every suspect Grey Goose bottle with a small black dot. I knew they were filled with Smirnoff, and I knew exactly where they were.

"In fact," I told them, "there's one sitting on the shelf in the Lobby Bar right now."

I finished with the final blow: that I believe that the monthly liquor costs were being manipulated to disguise the sale of stolen alcohol adding that I suspected that Dick, with the help of McGillicuddy, was allowing Bob to take bottles out of the hotel. I told them that if they checked, they would see that the invoices don't match the physical inventory.

I then drove the point home by accusing them of complicity. Someone there had to be aware that it was almost impossible for liquor cost to remain constantly positive and hardly ever-fluctuate. Dick's operation has clearly been running for a long time.

Rosemary was now sitting with her knees together, wringing her hands and studying the pattern on the carpet. Adrian was clicking away at his computer keyboard and studying whatever was on his computer screen. I figured he was pulling up the beverage department Profit and Loss statement. Pierre was just staring at me in awe.

I loved working at the Regency and being part of the hospitality industry; it was now in my blood, and I was finally finding my footing and becoming a better leader. I refused to let it show but the situation stung. I knew I was about to be turned out, and beneath the hurt, I was angry.

Chapter 30

I put my notebook back in my breast pocket and reminded myself to take a breath. After a few seconds, Pierre cleared his throat.

"Well, AJ, we thank you for that information you've provided. We have channels in place to handle what you've reported and at this point, we only have your suspicions but we will look into it.

He shook his head, sucked his teeth, and loudly said, *"Dès que tu soupçonnes quelque chose, tu aurais dû faire un rapport official. Parce que sachez que c'est apre's coup! Comprende?"*

I stared at him blankly, until Adrian spoke up.

"He's saying he wished you would have made an official report to us as soon as you suspected something. With this being the first we've heard of your complaints, it just looks like you're trying to save face, but I can assure you, we'll do a departmental investigation.

Pierre said in English, "But that still doesn't change the fact that there was a call regarding a supposed threat of assault."

"I know what's coming next, so let's get on with it."

Rosemary cautiously got up from her chair, opened the manila folder, and pushed sheets of paper across Pierre's desk in my direction. "I'm sorry, AJ, but we will have to immediately terminate your employment." When I reached for the paperwork, she moved to stand behind Pierre.

"Those are the forms we are required to provide you as a separated associate. You'll find information regarding your right to appeal our decision through a third-party mediator. At a cost to you of course. There's also information regarding your right to file for unemployment, as well as how to purchase COBRA insurance since all your benefits will be canceled at midnight."

"In addition, you'll also see there's a check that represents one-and-a-half months of your salary and compensation for your unused vacation hours. We are sorry that things have taken a turn like this, but even inferred acts of violence toward another employee is grounds for immediate termination."

After looking at the check, I folded it in half and put it in my pocket. I ripped the other paperwork in half and dropped the sheets into a trashcan in-between the desks. When Adrian and Pierre stood, Rosemary cautiously took the long way around and moved to the office door. She opened it and in stepped the hotel security chief, McGillicuddy, who was looking straight at me.

Rosemary, still keeping a safe distance, said, "Sean, would you escort AJ to the associate exit, please? He's to leave the property immediately."

She said to me, "AJ, you are not to speak to anyone on your way off the property or enter the beverage department office. Any personal items you have left in the office or your locker will be mailed to you."

I was about to tell her instead of mailing anything to me she could stick them up her ass, but I didn't. Instead I said, "I feel sorry for you all and anybody who has to work with Dick. He's a terrible person and an even worse leader."

McGillicuddy began walking in my direction. He was about a foot from me when he reached out as if he was going to take me by the arm.

I moved my right foot back, adjusted my balance and said, "If you touch me, I guarantee you it won't turn out the way you think."

He stopped dead in his tracks and looked to Rosemary for direction, but before she could say anything, Adrian stepped between him and me.

He placed his arm around my shoulder and said, "Rob, I'll escort him out. Come on, AJ, walk with me." I tensed under his touch but let him lead me out the door.

Adrian led me through the executive offices with his arm around my shoulder like we were old friends. Behind us, McGillicuddy said in a gruff voice, "Adrian, make sure he gets immediately off the property."

When I tried to turn around and go back toward him, Adrian tightened his grip on my shoulder and whispered to me, "Be cool, AJ, he's just trying to get your goat so he can call the police on you. Just walk with me man."

Once we were out of the executive offices I moved to go toward the employee exit, but Adrian turned and guided us in the opposite direction. Smiling, he said, "AJ, that door is for associates, and you're no longer employed here. You get to use the guest exit."

 As we walked across the Lobby, Adrian said, "AJ, I'm sorry about what happened in there. It was really out of my hands, but the way you stood up for yourself was impressive. Rosemary is normally fearless and reduces people to bowls of Jell-O, but today, she looked defeated."

When I stayed silent he continued, "You may not believe me, but Pierre and I had plans for you here. We knew you were having a hard time with Dick and we were impressed by the way you were enduring, but after that hotline call, your termination was out of our hands."

"We fought tooth and nail to get you that month-and-a-half severance pay because we think you deserve it. I'm sorry it didn't work out, but believe me, we will immediately do a deep dive into the beverage department's financials. We were both getting suspicious at the numbers and fed up with Dick's antics. There's a department audit coming and your ex-boss will have some explaining to do."

We were now standing on the sidewalk under the awning of the hotel's main entrance. I turned to

Adrian and said, "I appreciate you and Pierre fighting for me. I really did like this job but the truth is, I couldn't have put up with Dick much more."

"I understand, AJ. I'm sorry I couldn't do more sooner. I've been in this industry for over ten years, and we need more people like us in positions of leadership. Hiring you was the start of me doing my part to help with that, and I'll tell you a secret that may help you make a decision with your next job move."

Interested now, I looked at him expectantly for whatever words of encouragement he could share.

"I like being in a leadership position and working in management. Yeah, it comes with a lot of extra shit, but if I had it to do all over, I would just tend a bar. You've seen how Bartenders work their asses off, but they work fewer hours, aren't burdened with unmanageable expectations, and in the right environment, they can make more money than most managers. It might be something to think about AJ. Your work-life would be so much easier."

He handed me his business card, grinning. "Thanks for doing a good job for us. You can use Pierre and me for job references. Best of luck to you."

I was about to say something to him, but was interrupted by the sound of a vehicle pulling into the valet area. It was a late-model silver two-door convertible Mercedes Benz. Even before the car came to a stop, the attendants on duty sprang into action. One attendant moved to open the driver's door but before he could get into position, Adrian cut him off.

He held out an assisting hand to the driver once the door opened. "Good afternoon, Ms. Robinson. Nice to have you back with us again. How was your drive from DC?"

I saw why he moved so fast. The woman unfolding herself from the Mercedes was a knockout—a thirty-something blonde in a black dress that fought a losing battle with her curves. Adrian didn't even look back before he vanished back into the hotel.

<u>**Chapter 31**</u>

Standing on the sidewalk alone now, it felt weird seeing the hotel from this perspective. From inside, I had always thought of it as shiny and gleaming, but now that I was looking at it from the front, I saw the realness of it. The building's exterior concrete facade looked stained, discolored, and in need of a fresh coat of paint. I had always thought the hotel was beautiful. Obviously, I had been wearing rose-colored glasses.

I'd put three blocks between me and the hotel before the blur of tears finally dimmed my vision. Standing on a corner I didn't recognize, I realized I didn't know where I was going.

Regaining my sense of direction, I contemplated calling Driver for a ride but decided to walk home instead, so I can use the time to get my head wrapped around the fact that I was now officially unemployed.

It was just past noon when I arrived home. Still in a daze, I changed clothes, pulled the check out of my pocket, put it in a zip lock baggie, and hid it in the freezer. I rolled a joint and took a good, long pull.

In my current state of affairs I needed it as a healing and soothing sacrament.

I strongly believed that weed was not a drug but possessed a healing power. I used it as vehicle to take me closer to God as well as a reward for successfully navigating the peaks and valleys of life. Today I especially needed its medicine.

Sitting in the garden-patio, I felt a twinge of PTSD moving in on me. It was looking for a breach in the wall, to get through. I knew the drill: one wrong move or decision and I'd be calling my VA shrink to help me out of the dumps.

So, I chose a different route to get away from where I could head. I self-medicated with some Zazen Breathing after a big toke of medicine. I counted. I exhaled. I inhaled and I counted. Until I lost count.

An hour later, I was feeling much better. I drank my last four beers doing salutes to ghosts-friends. Unfortunately, the wound of my termination was still raw and the whole situation kept trying to creep right back in my thoughts.

My current financial state wasn't too dire. I had the cash I had squirreled away, along with the severance check I just got so I had enough to pay two months' rent in advance if I needed to. I didn't like that idea though, as doing that would strain my savings and affect my life-operating budget. I would be forced to watch every penny until I found another job.

Working was my regularly main stay, all the way back to the Marine Corps, and now, without employment, my world felt wonky and off-kilter.

It was still early afternoon when I finished the last beer. Feeling no more pain, I went inside, switched off the lights, pulled the drapes and lay on the couch. Tears ran down my face as I fell asleep.

Chapter 32

My head was throbbing when I woke up. I unfolded my body from the couch and tried to focus my vision on the only light in the room, the oven clock. It was 12.30 a.m.

I had a quick shower and my queasy stomach reminded me that I had not eaten. I had enough ingredients to make a grilled cheese sandwich, so I decided on that. While training in the Regency kitchens, I had learned the trick of substituting mayonnaise, instead of butter to crisp the bread slices.

I found a can of chicken noodle soup and poured it into a sauce pan, and put water on for tea. When the bread was toasty with the cheese oozing and the soup was bubbling, I plated and bowled up my dinner.

After I ate, I went outside to enjoy the patio-garden. It was so quiet that I heard the weird noises coming from the alley. It was coming from the aluminum trash cans being jostled around.

Every once in a while, people dug through the trash cans for recyclables along the alleyway, but never at this hour. Plus, the City had picked up trash earlier that morning. I did remember seeing cats, dogs, raccoons, and opossums along these streets and alleyways.

In fact, one night, I was sure I saw a coyote trotting down the middle of the next street over. It was most likely just rats out there, fighting over some spilled garbage. Whatever *it* was, as long as *it* stayed outside the walls, I'd continue to mind my business.

After getting myself some more water, and settling in again, the noises increased. I went over and looked into the security mirror outside the gate, and confirmed my suspicions about the noise. Rats were scurrying in, out and around the trash cans, almost like they were hunting something. That's when I heard a faint hiss, and a yowl.

As I listened, I was content to stay on my side of the fence, until the memory of Dick's bullying flashed in my mind, and I was mad all over again. Whatever the rats were after out there was most likely helpless and about to be dinner. I decided, I was getting involved.

Inside, I put on a pair of jeans and slipped my feet into my boots, and prepared a long-distance weapon. I removed a street broom that had been in my utility closet since I moved in, and unscrewed the pole from the brush section. Using black electrical tape, I attached my oldest steak knife on the end of the pole to create a spear. Quietly removing the locks on the gate, I eased it open and slowly snuck out.

I stood still allowing my eyes to adjust to the muted light. After confirming that no one was in the alley but me, and my homemade lance, I moved to where I saw the rats. They were still running around excited, then one suddenly popped onto the lid of one of the cans. It sat up on its hind legs, and daringly stared at me while sniffing the air and baring its teeth. It was as big as my foot, and I wear size twelve.

I rewarded his boldness by stabbing him in the chest. He struggled against the spear, and when I was certain he was skewered, I turned and flung him down the alley where he landed with a dull whap and did not budge. I then knocked on the cans, the sound loud in the quiet, and his cousins retreated in every direction.

Out of curiosity, I used the broom handle to wedge the cans apart. When I moved the third can, I stared down at a dirty ball of fur about the size of a coffee mug.

At first glance, I wasn't quite sure what I was looking at, so cautiously, I took the broom handle and wedged the cans apart even farther to get a better look. Huddled tightly in the gap and peeking up at me was a tiny kitten, and it was trembling.

It looked at me then took tentative peeks around the cans to check for its assailants. Not seeing any of the rats, it mewed weakly and inched slowly out. I saw that it was wary of me, so I made no sudden moves. When it got close to me, I bent, picked it up, and held it out into the alley lights so I could get a better look at it.

The kitten was so filthy I could only guess that it was orange in color, and it stunk to high heaven. Like speaking to a small child, I asked the kitten, "What are you doing out here by yourself?" I looked around the alley to see if a mama cat was near but only saw the rats moving down the alley on to new hunting grounds. If I left this baby out here, the rodent brigade would return and make a meal of it, so I took it inside.

I placed the kitten on a small end-table near the door and filled a plastic bowl with water for it. It sniffed the water then drank hungrily. I then examined it for wounds, but its fur was too filthy and matted to see anything. I needed to give it a bath.

The kitten explored a little while I went into the bathroom. I pulled a small plastic tub from under the sink and filled it with warm water. I poured in a few caps of isopropyl alcohol, squirted a few globs of my Herbal Essences shampoo, and went back for the kitten.

Using my softest washcloth, as gentle as I could be, I placed it in the water and washed it from head to tail. It didn't like it, but the bath definitely helped.

As I rinsed it, I noticed that is was male and the left ear would not stand up as the right ear did. I also noticed that left eye was barely open. I could see no cuts or scratches near the eye and when I put my finger close to it, the kitten didn't flinch.

Finished with the bath, the kitten purred as if grateful to be out of the water. It meowed and rubbed itself against me as I dried it off. I put it on the floor while I opened a can of tuna onto a paper plate. I sat the tuna in front of the kitten, and with a quick sniff, it ate like it had been starving. After it had its fill of tuna and water, I took it out onto the patio where it cautiously explored. Then, in one of the empty plant boxes, it dug out a little patch of dirt and promptly took a poop.

Chapter 33

As I watched the kitten I wondered what to do
with it. I didn't know anyone that I could give it to,
so maybe caring for this kitten would offset the
sadness and depression bearing down on me.

After about five minutes of contemplation, it
looked like I now had a roommate. I made a
mental checklist of what accessories I'd need for
my new ward.

My own needs were minimal and even
unemployed, I knew I could afford the extra
expense of having a pet. I said to the kitten, "I
wonder if you know how lucky you are. In fact,
cat-cat, that's your name: Lucky."

It was almost 3:30 a.m. when I took another quick
shower. I put Lucky on a pillow on the couch and
climbed into my bed. Before I fell asleep, I decided
not to inform the landlord about the kitten. It
wasn't like I was hiding a noisy puppy. Plus, how
much damage could a cat do?

I woke up to the strong smell of soap and
shampoo, and found Lucky asleep on my chest. I
had no idea when he had snuck in the bed with
me, but he was laying on his side with his head

resting near my chin, breathing into my neck. His weight felt so good on my chest, that for a while, I laid as still as possible so I didn't wake him. Finally, I reached over and turned on the lamp next to my bed. I stretched his ear to see if it would stay straight, but it flopped back to its bent position. I examined the pads of his feet, pressed out his little claws, and peeked at the eye that wouldn't stay open. The eyeball didn't move. It was milky white, and seeping a little. It was going to need some medical attention.

I carefully moved Lucky off my chest and went into the kitchen to make some coffee. A few minutes later, he sauntered out of the bedroom, ignored me, moved to the hallway door, and meowed. When I opened it, he first took a cautious look outside and went to handle his business. After I went inside to handle my own morning constitution, with a fresh cup of Joe, I went back outside for a smoke.

To test whether Lucky wanted to stay with me, I opened the patio-garden gate. As I held the gate open, Lucky took one look out into the alley, turned, and sauntered back into the apartment. I locked back the gate and followed him inside.

In the local phonebook, I searched for a veterinarian. I found The Village Vet & Pet Shop and it was only five blocks away. I dressed and took out some cash from my hidey-hole. When I went to get Lucky, it was as though he knew what my plans were, and ran and hid under the couch. After a few minutes of unsuccessfully trying to coax him out, I upended the couch, grabbed him, and we headed to the vet.

Lucky wasn't too happy about our journey, but I didn't have a whole lot of sympathy for him as I was also unhappy. Since I'd woken up I'd been fighting back thoughts of what happened at the Regency. It was still floating right there on the edges.

A few feet into our trip through the alley, we came upon the body of the rat I had stabbed. I didn't feel bad about killing it. Something had already eaten off its rear legs and I figured by tonight it would be finished off, and the circle of life would complete.

As we passed the rodent corpse, Lucky mewled and became antsy in my arms. The sight of one of my murdered adversary and the stink of the alley was even having an effect on me because I felt myself grinding my teeth and my anger returning.

The lyrics to Ella Fitzgerald's *"On the Sunny Side of the Street"* popped into my head. It made me feel a little better. We exited the alley to Bolton Street's red bricked sidewalk and made sure to walk where the morning sunshine was beating down on us.

 When we entered the Vet & Pet Shop, an electronic bell dinged announcing our arrival. No other customers were there yet. Then suddenly a twenty-something-aged white girl, with a septum piercing and blue-tinged hair faded on both sides, popped her head up from the other side of a shelf.

With a wide smile she welcomed us and just as she was about to say something else, she saw the bundle of fur in my arms. Almost running toward us, she said, "Aaaww! Look at your baby. Can I hold it?"

"Of course," I said and passed the kitten to her.

As the blue-haired girl took Lucky in her arms and rubbed him up against her cheeks, she seemed familiar, but I couldn't place her. She held Lucky up and looked underneath, then passed him back to me. "He looks good, except that eye thing. Where did you get him?"

"I rescued him from the alley behind my apartment last night. Some rats were about to kill it. I didn't see a mama around, so I guess I'm responsible for him now."

"So, you need to see the vet. We just opened and she should be here in a few. You all are first up."

Fifteen minutes later, Lucky was being examined. The veterinarian introduced herself as Anna. She'd taken over the practice from her father who'd run it for thirty-five years. Anna was short, in her fifties, and smelled of patchouli, and faintly of weed. I liked her right off the bat. She prodded, poked, pulled, and examined Lucky from head to tail.

"Considering he's from a feral colony, he's pretty healthy. He'll need to be neutered, and the only problem I see is that eye. He'll get no use out of it, it has no reaction to touch or light. I recommend we remove it before it becomes cancerous. The other eye is healthy, and he'll grow into only having the one. I also want to warn you that he'll be different than a normal domestic cat. Don't be discouraged if he's standoffish. Eventually he'll imprint on you in his own time."

Anna said that she could do the vaccinations, neutering, and eye removal the same evening but I'll need to leave him. If everything went well, I could pick him up tomorrow morning.

While I was thinking about how much the kitten was already cutting into my freezer-hidden savings, after only having it less than 12 hours, Anna was pointing at my eagle, globe, and anchor tattoo on my left forearm.

"Looks like you're a veteran, so you're in luck. The city has a program that helps veterans with health care for their pets. You just have to fill out a form, provide a copy of your veteran ID, and you only pay 25% of the cost."

When she left us in the exam room to print out the form, I breathed a sigh of relief for the good news of the city's financial assistance. Lucky shivered, so I cradled him in my arms and told him he'd be fine and I'd be back for him.

Anna came back and told me that after the city discount my responsibility would be $125.00. I agreed to the cost and she gave me the form to fill out. She took Lucky from me and promised they'd take good care of him.

After filling out the form I shopped for kitten supplies. As the young girl cashed me out, she must have seen something on my face. "Don't worry, they'll take good care of your new baby."

When she finished entering everything into the system, she said, "I'm giving you my family and friends discount, so your total will be even less."

"Thank you, that was nice of you." I wondered why she would be giving out her discount to a total stranger.

"Your name is AJ, right? You don't recognize me, do you?"

I stared at her, trying to place where I knew her from but came up empty. "No, I'm sorry. I don't."

"We're neighbors! My name is Robin. I live above you. I was sitting in my window the other day after your lady-friend left your place."

I was a little embarrassed I hadn't recognized her. "Oh shit, sorry! Small world."

"No worries. Sometimes we hear you down in your place, but with our schedules, we never got a chance to formally introduce ourselves."

"No problem. We'll have to hang out and all of us can properly meet like neighbors do. Plus, the other two ladies can meet Lucky."

Chapter 35

When I made it back to Bolton Street, I saw a dark grren Chevy van parked outside the girls' front door. It had started out as a passenger-conversion-style van, but now it was somebody's filthy work horse. The driver was pretty bold or just an asshole, because the trashy van was facing the wrong direction.

When I got to my gate, I heard someone moving around in the patio and no one was supposed to be in there. I reached for my knife as I unlocked the locks and pushed the gate open.

I took a few steps into the patio and saw a white guy in a gray jumpsuit bent over an AC unit. He had his back to the gate, and glanced in my direction when he heard the gate close, then he went back to fiddling with the AC unit. He had a cigarette dangling from the corner of his mouth and tools were scattered on the ground around him. I immediately didn't like this guy.

When I was almost standing over him, he said, "Hey buddy, I'm trying to fix this thing for the girl upstairs. I come down here for more room to work."

I glanced up at the second floor and saw that the door and window were both open.

Looking back down at him, I saw that there was an empty beer can and a few cigarette butts on the ground where he was working. "No problem man, just clean up after yourself when you finish."

He mumbled something as I unlocked my door and went inside. I thought it was rude that he didn't even introduce himself.

Inside the apartment, someone had pushed my mail under the door. As I skimmed through the stack of mostly junk mail, I saw a manila envelope from Hospitality Pro Search. I tore the envelope open and found an application and a background check authorization form, along with a self-addressed envelope. There was also a thank you note from Rachel and her request to fill out and return the forms as soon as possible. They were having in-person interviews in two weeks.

I knew the recruiter's call and these forms were a blessing in disguise, so I sat at the breakfast bar and filled out the paperwork. I used Adrian and Abyasa as references.

On my way out to the mailbox down the street, I passed the repair guy struggling up the back steps with the AC unit. He looked like he could use some help, but I ignored him.

When I got back, the workman was gone but he hadn't cleaned up his butts or the beer can. I knew I didn't like that guy for a reason. I swept up his leftovers and went inside.

About an hour later, my stomach growled reminding me that I had not eaten, so I closed the apartment again and hiked down to our neighborhood diner. It was a nice little place with friendly staff and good comfort food. I ordered a burrito with a cheesy sour cream sauce, a side of grits and, an order of sweet plantains, cranberry juice, and a chai latte. I dined while perusing the *City Paper*'s Help-Wanted section, then walked back home.

With not much else to do, I decided to spend some time giving my small apartment a good clean. With the radio on blast, my last task was now to scrub out the claw foot tub. While I scoured, I envisioned being in it with Ronnie. I thought about calling her, but was embarrassed to have to explain getting fired. Plus, sex with her again might be like opening Pandora's Box, so I shot down that idea.

As I rinsed out the tub, I received a message on my pager that read: *Hi Mr. Porter. This is Anna at Village Vet. I was calling to say everything went well with Lucky's operation. We'll observe him for the rest of the day, and you can pick him up tomorrow morning. We'll see you then*!

That afternoon, I realized that I needed something to do to keep my mind off of the shame of falling into Dick's trap and being fired. So, I packed my backpack with a copy of my resume' and Moleskin notebook and headed out.

On North Avenue, I caught the bus to the Pennsylvania Avenue branch of the Enoch Pratt Free Library. I got myself a library card, registered to vote, and prowled the stacks. After a while I set up at a computer and got to work. A few hours later, I had a brand-new résumé with only minor embellishments, a stack of graphic novels, and a book called *Invisible Life* about men on the down low.

Chapter 36

On the bus ride back to the house, I get off at a Save A Lot for some groceries, then at the Korean restaurant next door to the market, I got an order of fried chicken and some pork dumplings with rice wine- vinegar dipping sauce. I took my food to-go and caught the next bus home.

The next morning I made a list of places to visit and put in applications. The Sheraton, Marriott and Renaissance Harbor Place hotels were up first. I was out the house by 8:15 a.m. and was finished by 11:15 a.m. I went home, changed clothes, and was at the Vet to pick up Lucky by noon.

Lucky was lethargic when they brought him out, a combined side effect of the medications from the eye surgery and vaccinations. The vet assured me he'd bounce back in a few hours, then handed over a bottle of medication for his eye and instructions for how to administer the drops. Since the eyelid sutures were absorbable, no removal was needed. I booked a follow-up visit, thanked her for saving my new kid, and headed out.

On the walk home with Lucky cradled in the crook of my arm, my mind drifted to Dick and what was happening in the beverage department. By the time I got home, I had to make myself stop thinking about it.

I broke out Lucky's new toys, but he didn't have the least amount of interest, and he barely sniffed at the food and fresh water out for him. I put him on the couch and he pulled his little body up into a corner, and fell asleep.

I was reading and watching over him when I heard steps on the stairs outside. I was sure it was the handyman again, so I went outside to tell him about leaving his trash the other day, but it was blue-haired Robin, followed by two other girls.

Smiling, Robin said, "Hey neighbor! I know your baby came home today, so I told the girls that we had a new housemate that just had an operation. So, we're coming for a quick visit. Plus, the asshole is back, so it's the perfect time for all of us to meet." I looked up and saw the same guy from yesterday fitting an AC unit into the window on the third floor.

The girls came down into the patio holding cans of beer. The heaviest girl of the trio came down last, and with a big smile, she handed a can to me and said, "I hope you drink beer, because we bought you one too. I'm Katie."

We shook hands and I said thank you and took the beer. The other girl was thin, and her skin was a darker complexion. She held out her hand to me and, with a Spanish accent, said, "Hi, I'm Elizabeth, everyone calls me Liz."

I got them lawn chairs from under the steps and opened them. Lucky heard the ladies and came out to investigate the new voices. I watched him like a parent as he sauntered out, turning his head side to side, practicing with his one eye. When he meowed, Robin saw him and jumped out of her seat and snatched him up like they were old friends.

For the next few minutes, I sipped my beer while Robin and Katie carefully passed Lucky back and forth giving him all the love. Liz just watched them as if she didn't like cats so when Katie placed him onto her lap, she stared down at him like she was appalled at first, but after he began purring and rubbing against her, she smiled and petted him. Robin even joked that his handicap would make him appear tough when he got bigger and told us about other people's pets with worse handicaps.

We were interrupted when the handyman called down from the third-floor window next to the now-installed AC unit. "Miss Katie, I got her working, but I have to go get some freon from the hardware 'round the corner. I'll be right back."

With a twinge of contempt, she said, "Okay, whatever." She turned to us. "I hope he hurries and gets out."

It felt good to have company. They took turns telling me about themselves and what kind of art they create. Robin was from Rochester, Katie was from Richmond, and Liz was from Madrid. I told them about myself, and before I could stop, I told them about the drama of my dismissal from the hotel. Katie and Robin expressed statements of empathy. Liz didn't say anything. She just had a strange look on her face.

We were talking about work when the AC window unit came to life. It ran for a few seconds, then the kitchen window opened, and the handyman's head and shoulders popped out.

He looked down at Liz. "It's all good now, Miss 'Lizbeth. I got it in there good and tight, and I checked the others, and they good as well. I'll send your daddy my bill. I can let myself out. See you girls."

Liz half-heartedly nodded up in his direction, rolling her eyes. "Okay, Egbert. Just make sure the door is locked behind you, please."

Noticing how she spoke to the handyman, I flashed back to how she looked when I told them about not having a job. Right then it became clear—Liz's father was my landlord.

When the handyman pulled his head back in the window, Katie snorted into the air as she stood. "I'll go close up and make sure my panties are still there, and I'll bring fresh beers."

Chapter 37

A little embarrassed, Liz said to me, "I'm sure you heard him mention my father. My parents own this house. They bought it when I was a freshman, and my father got transferred to the States. My dad is the interior attaché at the Spanish Embassy down in DC. He used to commute back and forth every day, but he got tired of the Metrorail and spending a large part of his day riding a train. They kept this house and purchased a townhouse down in Georgetown. Now my mom gets more access to the in-crowd and my dad is closer to work."

Robin interjected, "We've all been best friends since boarding school, so it's easy to live together here instead of in those outdated, nasty-ass dorms … Yuck!"

I guessed that I was probably the only rent-paying tenant so I changed the subject and looked up at the newly installed window AC. "You all don't like that guy, huh?"

Just as Robin was going to say something, Liz loudly sucked her teeth. She gazed at me with her forehead creased with anger. "Yeah, he's the neighborhood fix-it dude and unfortunately, I had to have my dad call him because the central air system is not working. My dad even bought window units from him until we could get the central air fixed."

Liz looked at the main AC unit in the corner surrounded by a heavily padlocked steel cage. "But to answer your question, no. We don't like him. He's a fucking creep! I think he ripped my dad off because he said those units were in perfect working condition, but since he installed them a month ago, every one of them has had problems."

Robin jumped in. "Plus, every time he's here, he always acts so fucking pervish, and something is always missing after he's gone. One time when he was here fixing my bathroom sink, I'm pretty sure he stole a pair of my panties out of my dirty clothes bin."

Laughing, Liz chimed in, "He was probably destined to be a pervert from birth. Who the hell names their child Egbert and expects him to be normal?"

We were all laughing when Katie returned. She passed out beers, opened her bottle with a church key, and passed the bottle opener along. Robin opened hers, then mine and Liz's bottle. We all leaned forward, holding our bottles together. Katie said, "He's gone and everything's locked up." Before we toasted, she put up her index finger to stop our salute, then deftly produced a joint from the folds of her hair, smiling widely. "Now we can toast!"

I went to get us some leftover blackberry brandy I had stashed in the freezer, and a stack of Dixie Cups with Lucky trailing behind me. I returned just in time to catch the joint as it arrived at my spot. The ladies were now rehashing incidents about Egbert. They talked about how he always smelled like a drunk, his corny attempts at flirting, about him gawking at them, and how he constantly made sexual innuendos, and how things always ended up missing after he left. Apparently, he made them so uncomfortable, they made sure none of them were ever alone with him.

As I poured us hits of fruited liquor, we drank, talked, laughed, and got to know each other better, the mood was nice and mellow. Even Lucky came back out and was asleep in the crook of Robin's arm.

Later on, Katie and Robin wished me luck on my job hunt as they headed back up to their apartment, but Liz lagged behind.

Looking serious, and in her strong Castilian accent, she said, "It's very rare that that my father comes here, and I won't tell him, but he would not like that you have a pet and if he knew, he'd charge you extra. He will, however, immediately notice if he does not receive your rent payment."

Then she smiled and said, "Just so you know, we have always liked the idea of you—a man living here with us. We didn't even know you, but we felt safer. Please stay if you can and good luck with the job search. Also, if you ever need cat sitters because of a new work schedule, please let us know."

I smiled back at her and we shook hands.

I gathered the bottles and cups, emptied the ashtrays, put the lawn chairs away and went inside.

<u>**Chapter 38**</u>

Around nine-thirty the next day, a sudden vibration against my hip made my heart flip. I pulled the pager from my pocket, hoping for Ronnie's name, but the screen displayed an unfamiliar number. The message scrolled across: *"You can meet me please at the Bill's Bar at two thirty p.m. today? Es importante, mi hermano. Es Vidal."*

My interest was piqued. There must be some shit going on at the hotel if he was paging me. Meeting up with him was now the main thing on my day's schedule.

After waking Lucky, who was now lounged on the top of the couch, I gave him the first of his daily eye washes, which became a battle that ended with us not being friends. I knew we'd stay that way until it was time to feed him.

I walked down the street to the corner box, bought *The Baltimore Sun*, and got the latest free copy of *The Other Paper*. Returning home, I opened both windows in my bedroom and the one in the kitchen to get some cross breeze flowing, then spent the morning perusing the local rag.

I circled a few jobs that sounded interesting and I thought might be a good fit for me, and because it was a nice morning, I immersed myself in some of *The Sun* articles.

I read about how people mourned the end of an era with the coming demolition of Memorial Stadium. Another story was about a writer named David Simon who had a new book coming out about his time embedded with the Baltimore Homicide unit for a year. He had plenty to write about with the almost constant citywide murders that were headed to over three hundred this year. Seventy-five percent of those would be young Black men involved in the drug trade.

I frowned through a long op-ed piece from some angry guy who claimed that Mayor Kurt Schmoke's re-election was rigged, and citywide gerrymandering was immediately needed. He claimed that the white vote would prove powerless and white people would disappear from their long held place of superiority in Baltimore.

I switched to *The Other Paper* and checked the arts, concerts, and events sections first. I flipped to the back pages to review the nasty-forward, downright-weird, sex-filled ads in the "personal and desperately seeking" sections. The soliciting, appeals, supplications, petitions, and invitations always made for interesting reading that was damn near pornographic.

At 1:00 p.m., I headed to the Inner Harbor to meet Vidal. On my ride, I kept myself entertained by the snippets of conversations I overheard on the bus, and enjoying the cityscape as we rolled.

Chapter 39

I was seated at the bar in Barnacle Bill's when Vidal showed up. He had a big smile on his face as we ordered drinks and got caught up on general things. We had become close enough that I'd come to not even notice his back-and-forth transition from English to Spanish. He, in turn, accepted my butchering of his native language with patient correction.

Getting to the reason he wanted to meet, he told me that my getting fired was the talk of the hotel and a lot of employees were "_Muy enojado, amigo_ … very angry."

He said people knew that Dick was the cause, and that Bob was _despedido_. When he said his name was _blacked out_ on the schedule, I assumed the English translation was that he had been _fired._

"AJ, people who asustado (fear) Dick before are fed up now. You were a _buen jefe,_ a good man, and peoples respect you. I ask Dick why you gone, and he tell me to mind my business or I will be next, so, I go to Adrian and tell him Dick threatens me."

As he spoke, he had a strange look on his face. I said, "*Mira, Vidal,* I appreciate you all caring, but please don't get yourselves caught in Dick's sights. He'll get you too."

When he made his next pronouncement, I understood that Vidal's previous strange look was the setup to what he had to say next. "*Jefe Adrian* take me to the HR. I tell the senora Rosemary what Dick say to me. Also, *hermano*, all the cocktail servers from the Lobby Bar, the waiters and bartenders from Poe's, the banquet bartenders, and even Ms. Theresa all go talk to her about him."

The conversation had now got real interesting. With the new flood of reported instances of Dick's rude and unprofessional behavior, within hours he was moved to a new position. By that afternoon, a new beverage manager from another Regency property had already been brought in to take his place

"AJ, but they don't fire that *pendejo*! He is moved to Valet Supervisor. Now, he park the autos."

I couldn't help but smile at the thought of Dick being knocked down a peg. Vidal grinned back, and started loading up his next punchline.

"*Mi amigo,* today he yelled at the valet chicos to say they lazy. Then they tell him to 'fuck off' and they quit. Then the Dick, he have to work solo." He rapidly said, "AJ, *lo veo sudar en su traje! Y tan pronto como entregaba un coche, agarraba más llaves y salía disparado por el garaje a por otro, con el brazo balanceándose.*"

I had to stop him, "*Too rapido...no entiendo, no comprende, hermano...* I don't understand!"

He nodded, and after searching for the English translation, he said, "Aaahhh." He laughed and switched to English. "After the valet chicos leave, him sweating out his suit. He deliver a car, then he grab more keys and take off at the garage for another and his arm swinging." He mimicked Dick's right arm swinging.

He told me that a line of angry guests stood in queue checking their watches and complaining about the long wait to get their cars. The backup got so long and became such a cluster fuck that Front Desk associates had to come help bail him out.

We both laughed at the visual image as he told the story, and tears ran from my eyes. I got the bartender's attention and ordered us a new round. We toasted to Dick's demotion.

Vidal floated the idea that maybe the Regency would rehire me, but I shot it down. That would require management to offer way too many explanations and, worse, admit they were wrong to fire me in the first place.

"Besides, I think I found a *nuevo trabajo.*"

He clapped me on the shoulder, *"Felicidad, hermano!"* and we toasted again.

We closed out our tab, and out on the sidewalk, we shook hands and man-hugged with the promise to stay in touch. Then he gave me a pack of Regency matches with a number written inside. He winked at me and said, *"Es from la niña Daniela.* She say give to you."

I was tempted to walk over to the hotel just to watch Dick struggle, but I knew that wasn't a good idea because I still felt like slapping the shit out of him. Knowing he was miserable and his money train had finally been knocked off the tracks was good enough for now.

Settling into an empty seat on the bus, I couldn't help but think Dick had no idea how fortunate he was to be dealing with a righteous man. I spent the ride thinking about karma and how it don't always come when you want it, but it always comes on time.

On my short walk home my pager vibrated with an incoming message. It was from the restaurant representative Rachel had told me about. The message said that over the next 3 days they were holding Open Interviews in a conference room at the Renaissance Hotel, and she wanted to know if I was interested in attending.

I called her back and agreed to an 11:00 am interview the following morning.

<u>Chapter 40</u>

I woke up excited for my interview. While I shaved and trimmed, I practiced answers to potential questions. I had planned to eat a light breakfast and relax a bit, but I needed to take care of Lucky's eye first. He was growing by the day and showing his personality and aversions more and more. This morning of all days, he decided that he was having no part of me messing with his eye. I finally wrangled him and got him to take the medicine.

After tussling with my feline child, I had no time for food and only had time to focus on assembling a job-procuring clothing ensemble. I outfitted myself in a cornflower-blue suit I had never worn and was saving for a special occasion. I chose a black Lycra T-shirt, a pair of royal-blue argyle socks, and my black three-quarter Chelsea boots.

Selecting accoutrements from the cigar box that held my few pieces of jewelry, I switched out my normal left-ear stainless steel hoop for a matte black one and chose a blue cat's-eye pinkie ring and a silver chain bracelet. I put on my dog tags under the T-shirt for good luck. I called Driver and he ferried me to the Inner Harbor.

At the hotel, I checked in and realized it was a group interview process. There was a lot of competition to work at this place; at least fifty other people waited for their chance to make an impression. From the time I was there, I only saw two other people of color waiting to interview, but I tried not to focus on the color imbalance and focused instead on getting that money.

When my name was called, and I stepped into the batter's box. I let my personality shine and sold myself on my military background and hospitality leadership experience. They were impressed when I talked about the training program I'd been through at the Regency. After a longer in-depth interview, I was offered, and accepted, the position of Bartender. I filled out employment documents, received an offer letter and left, floating on air.

I strolled into Barnacle Bill's and ordered a Dirty Gin Martini. I settled in, nursing my drink and a cigarette, before putting in a food order: a T-bone steak, scrambled eggs, cheese grits, onion rings, and a slice of key lime pie with blueberry compote.

I was startled a bit when a hand touched my shoulder. I turned, surprised to see Daniela sliding into the seat next to me. "Hey, AJ. You look sharp," she said, eyeing my clothes. "What's the occasion?"

We shared a brief greeting and then I told her about the new gig, and her face lit up. "That's great, AJ! To be honest, I don't usually come here, but Vidal mentioned I might find you here. I had some time before meeting a friend, so I figured I'd try to catch you. I wanted to see how you were holding up. I think what they did to you was terrible, and I really miss having you around. Plus, I wanted to fill you in on what's happening at work."

Her pronouncement kind of threw me. I tried to make sure I didn't blush, but looking at her, it was hard to not be captivated by her beauty. She looked stunning in a yellow crop top, a black jacket, and jeans so tight they looked painted on. Daniela definitely had the high voltage sexiness like Nia Long and Tyra Banks.

I offered her a drink, and she settled on a glass of Pinot Grigio. I asked the bartender to bag the rest of my food to go so I could focus on her. As we talked, Daniela kept either touching my forearm or tracing the veins on my hand with her red-lacquered nails.

"Everybody feels real bad about you getting fired. I heard what happened with Bob in the office. You should have kicked his ass!"

I grinned and said, "For a minute there, I thought we were going to fight but I'm glad it didn't happen otherwise I'd have been arrested."

Continuing to finger-trace the back of my hand, which I enjoyed, Daniela said, "I heard from my friend in accounting that after being demoted, Regency Corporate bought in auditors, and they investigated the beverage department's financials. They found all kinds of irregularities, all because of what you told management. When they questioned him about it, he tried to blame you, but Abyasa stepped up and told them that Dick did not allow you to be involved in anything financial related. Plus, a lot of the errors they found were from when you were no even working there yet."

She continued, "The next nail in his coffin was when those part-time Valets all quit-at the same time. After that, they brought in the corporate lawyers. They called him in for a meeting and after that, he resigned. I think he got a small severance, but it wasn't anything like what he would have gotten if he had quit after his accident."

I was a bit surprised by this news, happy that management actually looked into what I told them. I was sure Dick was running scared with the possibility of criminal charges looking over him.

Shaking my head I said, "No better for his ass!"

"I agree. So, can I buy you a drink now to celebrate?"

She ordered us Lemon Drop shots and excused herself to go to the restroom. As I watched her walk away I started thinking about the word *comeuppance*.

Over the last couple days, I'd been getting better at realizing that even though what happened to me was unfair, it may have been for the best. I was sure that increased disrespect from Dick would have ended with violence. The crazy Marine inside would have emerged, and there would be no putting that genie back into the bottle.

I blew a plume of smoke upward and smiled at the fact that my accidental discovery of his scheme had formed a snowball that bought the avalanche down on Dick's head.

Chapter 41

Daniela returned just as our shots arrived. As she settled in next to me she made sure to press her thigh against mine. She asked, "What you grinning about?"

"I was just sitting here thinking that no matter what happened, life is good."

We smiled, tapped glasses, and downed the lemony-sugary-fused vodka.

Looking at the time, I remembered Lucky was overdue for food and an eye rinse. "Hey Daniela, I gotta head out."

"Okay, my friend is on the way. Should be here in a few. Can you wait with me till then?"

"Of course."

After closing out my tab Daniela insisted on paying for the drink. I dropped some cash for my food and we stood out front of the restaurant, smoking.

She took my hand and grinned. "Vidal told me he gave you my phone number, and I expect to hear from you. At work, you were always so focused that I couldn't ever catch your eye. I know we weren't supposed to fraternize but now that you don't work there, I think it would be nice for us to get to know each other better and hang out sometime."

She leaned over, pressing her body against me, and gave me a lingering kiss on my lips. When she pulled back, she whispered in a husky voice. "Congratulations! That's for good luck on your new job, you're gonna do great."

With that, I promised to keep in touch. Just as she pulled away, I heard the sound of Michael Jackson's voice blaring *Remember the Time.*

A shiny, candy-apple-red Toyota Supra pulled to the curb in front of us. When it came to a stop, I noticed that Daniela had taken two steps away from me. The car looked showroom new, and the T-tops were open and the driver's eyes rested on me. He didn't look happy.

The guy was slim and his skin was the color of a brown paper bag. He was a pretty man trying hard to look cool but his whole outlook bordered on comical.

He wore brown leather driving gloves, the same color as the Toyota's faux leather interior, and was sporting an S-curl-high-top fade with aviator sunglasses that had yellow lenses.

He was dressed in a long sleeved white polo shirt with an alligator on the left breast, shiny black jeans with a sharp crease, and a canary-yellow cardigan sweater that hung over his shoulders. The arms were tied in a square knot on his chest.

When Daniela stepped forward, he put the car in park, grabbed the top of the partial roof, and stood. He leaned over and said, "What's the haps, lover?" Instead of leaning down and opening the door for her, he poked out his lips in a pucker for a kiss.

Daniela scrunched up her forehead. "Hey Leslie" and instead of kissing his lips, she gave him a quick peck on the cheek. Looking disappointed, he rolled his eyes at me and flopped back down into the driver's seat.

Opening the passenger door herself, Daniella said, "This is my cousin AJ. He's the one I was telling you about that used to work at the Regency with me. Is it alright if we give him a ride home, please? We have plenty of time to make our reservation."

He looked up at me, glowering at my outfit and with a sneer, he said, "Yeah, long as I don't have to go into the 'hood'. I'm not taking my car to the ghetto."

Daniela held the door open and leaned the front seat forward for me to climb in. Grinning at me, she said, "Come on, cousin! I told you he would be cool with it."

After squeezing into the tiny backseat, I said, "Nice to meet you, man and thanks for the ride, but I don't live in the hood. Just over on Bolton Hill. I hope that doesn't take you too much out of your way."

He grunted something and as Daniela buckled up, he pulled off into traffic. For the rest of the ride, they bickered up front and seemed to forget I was in the backseat. I couldn't really hear what they were saying because music was screaming out of the speakers again.

When the song that was playing ended, "*Black or White*" started up just as loud. It was a cool song and all but why was this guy really riding around, blasting music like there was no tomorrow!

I decided at that moment that I didn't like Daniela's friend. He seemed like an asshole and a show off. He drove too aggressively, and I didn't like the way he spoke to her.

Two blocks from my apartment, I couldn't take anymore. I leaned between the bucket seats and said, "Excuse me you all, but right here'll be fine for me to get out."

He promptly slammed on the brakes causing us all to lurch forward. Daniela gave him a dirty look.

She got out and leaned the seat up, and as I scooted out, she grazed the top of my hand with her red-lacquered fingernails again. She whispered, "Don't forget me, cousin."

When she got back in and was seated, I shut her door then I purposely walked in front of the car so he couldn't pull off. Standing over him at his driver's window as he grimaced up at me, I took a ten-dollar bill out of my pocket and dropped it into his lap. When he looked down to see what I'd given him, I clapped him hard on the shoulder and said, "Thanks for the ride. That's for your trouble, Lester."

He burned rubber as they pulled away from the curb and over the loud sound of Michael Jackson singing '*Dangerous*' I heard him tell Daniela, "Your cousin better get it right! My name ain't no fucking Lester. It's Leslie!!"

I walked home in high spirits, mainly because of having a new job but also because of the sheer comedy of gaining a new cousin.

Chapter 42

The next morning, I was out in the patio garden having my morning coffee and a cigarette when I realized that the house above me was afire with commotion. It sounded like all three girls were awake and moving around furniture. I heard Robin yell, "When did you last see it?"

There was no answer but then Katie chimed in. "Girl, you probably just misplaced it somewhere."

Catching her accent, I heard Liz shout, "No! I always put it back in the same place!"

It was so loud upstairs that when I went back inside, Lucky was staring at the ceiling of our apartment. While I poured a top-up for my coffee, we heard drawers and doors slamming and then cursing. As I came back outside, Liz was coming down the stairwell. She opened a lawn chair, plopped down next to me, and put her head in her hands.

"Ahhh, good morning. What's wrong?" I asked.

She sighed, then started sobbing.

I let her cry while I went inside to get some paper towels. As she dried her tears I waited for her to tell me what was wrong. Through her tears, and dripping mucus, she told me.

"I can't find my necklace. It's a really important family heirloom. After Spain's Civil War in 1930s, my great-grandfather was a soldier and was awarded the Laureate Plate of Madrid medal for his acts of bravery in protecting his fellow citizens. When the war ended, he left the military and was the first person in his family and village to go to university. For good luck, he took the medal off its ribbon and hung it on an eighteen-karat gold rope."

She paused to wipe her face. "Later, he passed it down to my grandfather when he left for college. Then my grandfather gave it to my dad and two years ago, right before I started art school, my dad gave it to me, and now it's gone!"

Liz dried her tears again and sniffled. "My father made an appointment for me to take it to his insurance agent on Monday morning to have it appraised and insured and If I tell my parents, they're gonna freak out and it'll confirm everything they have already been worried about, that Baltimore is too crime-ridden and I shouldn't live here alone. When he finds out he'll sell this house and make me move down DC."

In a hard voice she said, "I just know it was stolen because I wear it several times a week and I don't just leave it laying around, and I know it was that fucking Egbert that took it. I'm sure of it!"

Trying to reassure her, I said, "I'm sure it'll show up. Just wait before telling your dad."

"Thanks for being optimistic, AJ but we've searched everywhere in this house! When I opened my jewelry box this morning, it was gone. The last time I saw it was when he was here fixing the AC the other day. I was going to take it to school today and have my friend, who creates jewelry, clean it for me so it'd look nice."

She broke down sobbing again. Lucky came out and meowed at her feet. She picked him up, petted him, and that calmed her down some.

As she stroked Lucky, he wallowed in her arms, and I felt a pang of jealousy. Even though I saved his life, gave him medical care, and provided food and shelter, he was still a bit standoffish with me. The best signs of affection I got from him was when he'd wait at the inside apartment door when I returned home or when I woke up with him asleep in the crook of my arm.

After she composed herself a little, I asked, "Are you sure you just didn't misplace it somewhere?"

She shook her head. "The girls want me to call the police and make a report, but I have no proof. Plus, if my father finds out, we'll all have to move. Me to Washington, and Katie and Robin into the dorms. I know Egbert lives near here but I don't know where, or I'd go to his house, tell him I know he stole it, and demand he give it back!" Then she went back to blubbering again.

I felt bad for her and the other girls. Liz wanted no part of living down in the Nation's Capital with her parents, and Robin made it clear that she and Katie detested the idea of having to move into the art institute's campus housing.

I had a mental image of Egbert creeping through the ladies' space, fingering their underclothes while rummaging for valuables to steal. A gut feeling told me that he'd snatched the medal the day we'd all been hanging out below.

Liz calmed down a bit more and said, "Thanks for listening AJ. I have to get ready for class."

She placed Lucky on the chair and trudged up the stairs sniffling. I knew right then that if the opportunity presented itself, I was going to get Egbert.

Chapter 43

A couple of hours later, the high wore off. My new GM called with bad news: construction delays had pushed back training indefinitely. He promised to touch base in a few days with a new start date so suddenly, my schedule was wide open again.

Neither my library books nor the static on the TV could hold my interest for long so I called Daniela as promised. She didn't pick up so I hung up without leaving a message.

Once the girls left for school and their chatter faded, I was left alone with the heavy silence of the house.

The silence finally got to me. Unable to sit with my own company and a cat any more, I headed out to Mount Vernon for lunch. As I walked, the Italian-influenced architecture caught my eye and I noticed the occasional row house that was converted into a business of some sort.

Just like back in Bolton Hill, these little mom-and-pop shops felt strangely out of place—as if a cyclone had plucked them up and dropped them right into the middle of a residential block.

Turning corners with no set direction in mind, I explored places I always wanted to see and came up on a block that I'd never been on before. Directly across the street were three buildings close together. There was a small deli on the first corner, and next to that was an old-school pharmacy, followed by a print and photo developing shop. There was a narrow alley after that shop which lead to the back of the buildings.

Over the first door on the other building there were two signs. It looked like house that had been converted into a business place. Adjoining that was a bail bondsman's office. The last structures looked like two residential buildings but the one close to the alley was abandoned.

My belly growled and I was about to cross the street to the deli when I noticed a van that looked very similar to Egbert's. It was parked a few spots away from where I was standing.

I slowly made my way to it and realized that is was the same van that was at our house. I came abreast of the front fender and slyly touched the front grill. It was hot, meaning it was recently parked and the driver was somewhere on this area and I think I had an idea where to look first.

Right across the street, on the transom above the entryway to the bodega, in hand-painted block letters a sign read: *Mt. Vernon Dew Drop Inn, Tavern and Sundries*. I crossed the street and entered the portal into the small store. Off to the right of the entryway a door stood ajar; I assumed it led to the tavern.

I went to the counter and ordered a pack of Kool's, a bottle of RC, and a roll of Life Savers.

As I was paying for my items I asked if the bar was open. The cashier eyed me suspiciously and the whole time his right hand was hidden below the counter. I was sure it was gripped around some sort of weapon. In a voice as dry as bone, he said, "Bar's always open."

I peeked my head into the tavern and there was Egbert, just as I expected, sitting at the bar with a group of people. No one noticed me when I slipped inside.

The bar was old and I imagined that whoever owned it most likely lived upstairs. Neon beer signs and aged framed photographs hung on the walls, which were made of old wood, just like the floors. The whole room smelled like cigarette smoke and pine cleaner.

The most modern things in the place were a 1970's Clint Eastwood Dirty Harry pinball machine and a Wurlitzer jukebox that accepted nickels, dimes and quarters and played forty-five records.

I slowly made my way to the end of the bar and got the bartender's attention. "Hey, can I get change for a dollar?"

While he got my change, I slyly watched the group through the mirrored back wall of the bar. The group at the bar talked and paid me no attention. It was like I wasn't even there.

There was an antique phone booth in the corner with an accordion door and a red cushioned seat. I quietly made my way to it and left the two-section accordion glass door slightly open. I could hear the group's conversation clearly from here.

I dropped a quarter in the slot and took a seat. Dialing my answering service, an operator picked up after two rings. "Thank you for calling Utilix Communication. How can I assist you today?"

"Checking for messages, please." I gave her my seven-digit account number and security code.

At the bar, the bartender stocked a cooler and the group listened to Egbert. The operator said, "You have no new messages." and I broke the connection, but I continued to hold the receiver to my face, pretending that I was still on the line.

I heard Egbert say to the group, "I tol' you. She said she ain't had no money and I wuzn't working for free, so she gave me this!"

My spot in the phone booth provided a great reflection of what he was doing through the mirror in the back of the bar. I could see him showing something to the group. It looked like a medal, and I was sure it was Liz's great-grandfather's necklace.

With a shit-eating grin, he told the group that tomorrow he was going to take it to a pawn shop where he knew he would get a good bit for it

I dropped another quarter in the slot and called my home phone. My answering machine came on, and I spoke to Lucky. I knew he could hear me through the speaker. "What you doing, kid?"

Egbert said, "I'gotta go, y'all. I got a job to finish over at the printers. Den later tonight, I'ma meet two Pig Town strippers right here. We gon' drink some fancy vodka that I came across, so maybe I'll get lucky and we'll have us one of them menagary-twats!"

One of the ladies in the group muttered, "You're still ignorant as ever!"

"That might be, but I ain't never knowed them fancy words like you, but you know what? I'ma still get laid two times tonight!" He laughed at his joke and the other patrons just shook their head at him.

I ended my call and slipped out of the booth unseen and hurried out the bar.

I quick-stepped to the next block, stopped, and looked back in the direction of the bar, memorizing the street layout. That was when I heard a voice and turned to see a woman coming my way. It was obvious that the chemicals in the dope she ingested had gotten ahold of her, so it was hard to discern her age or even her race. She came and stood next to me, studying me up and down.

She said, "Hey man, you got a square I can have?"

I fished a cigarette out of my pack and gave it to her.

After lighting it, she upped the ante. "Do you have any money to spare?"

I reached into my pocket and gave her the two quarters I and left. She frowned and spat on the sidewalk at my feet.

Through brown-stained teeth, she said, "Tha's it? What you even doin' 'round here? You 'ont live on dis street! You need to get your ass on away from here!" Then she slithered down the sidewalk without even a 'thank you'.

When I looked back at the bar, a man stood outside the bail bond office, looking in my direction. Even as I walked off, I could feel him staring at me.

Chapter 44

Back on my side of Bolton Hill, I stopped at the market and bought a pack of chicken, a bottle of Sauvignon Blanc, and a tin of Monte Cristo cigarillo. After cleaning and marinating the chicken, out on the patio I got out my little hibachi grill and got it going. While reading *The Choirboys* by Joseph Wambaugh, Lucky had caught a water bug and was giving it hell.

Just before the meat was ready, I headed inside to make a salad, tossing romaine and spring mix into to a Tupperware bowl along with an aggressive medley of heirloom tomatoes, golden beets, jalapeños, and sliced strawberries.

Once the grilled chicken had rested, I diced it up and added it to the mix, hitting the whole mess with lemon juice, red wine vinaigrette, and a handful of garlic croutons. I snapped the Tupperware lid shut, gave it a shake, and ate it right out of the bowl with and Triscuits that I dipped in blackberry jam. I paired my meal with a glass of wine.

I cleaned the kitchen then had a little cigar on the patio with a book while Lucky napped on the chair next to me. When it started to get dark, I got up and gathered up my stuff. Lucky peeled open his good eye, stretched, and let out a little meow, then followed me inside.

I was in the bed by 7:35 p.m. but I was only going down for a nap. Before I fell asleep I thought about the plan I had formulated.

I woke up a few hours later with Lucky curled up in the crook of my right arm as usual. He was having a nightmare because he extended and retracted his claws into my forearm as he made little cat sounds. I'd seen dogs when they had nightmares, but this was my first time for a cat. He didn't break my skin, so I didn't wake him. I just gently stroked him until he calmed down.

If I was going to get Liz's necklace back, the first thing to do was confirm if Egbert lived on that block and if he did, then I had to be ready to take action. I got up and started getting dressed.

I donned a pair of black cargo pants, a black T-shirt, and my black jungle boots. I completed my sable outfit with a reversible black hoodie, tying a black bandanna around my neck and a pair of black leather driving gloves. I put my aluminum penlight in my left cargo pocket, I slipped the leather sap into my back pocket. I had three different sized Ka-Bar knives and I chose the smallest one that measured 7" with the sheath. I clipped that one onto my belt inside my pants. In the half mirror I looked over my outfit and was happy with what I saw. I was ready.

At 11:01 p.m. I exited the apartment and silently padded down the now empty streets. As my eyes adjusted to the varying levels of light I was being careful not to trip in any potholes or the general unevenness of the cobblestone sidewalks. So far, I was moving along stealthily and the only witnesses to my campaign were dogs tied up in backyards that barked and snarled as I passed.

They say you can tell what type of people live in a neighborhood by the type of cars you see around. I didn't believe that because I passed every year, make, class, style, and model of. The only thing I could discern, was that parking was at a premium and some drivers couldn't parallel park to save their lives.

I'd once read an article in *The Atlantic* magazine that claimed wealthy people were prone to exposing their lives for display. I don't know if that was true, but I passed a lot of homes where the blinds were open. I could see into a lot of homes without even trying. Some of these residences were so visually accessible that they had to have been staged on purpose.

I'd even heard about people who got off on the idea that someone *might* be watching them. It must be true, because some of those homes I passed, I saw people in various stages of undress. After a few blocks, I crossed the street whenever I saw windows with unhindered views, just in case a voyeur was watching for a viewer.

Further along the cobblestone sidewalk in front of me, was a white Volkswagen that was bouncing up and down. It was parked at the curb behind a line of other vehicles. All the windows were down and it was parked only a few feet from the front steps of homes. The little German car's suspensions were being put through its paces because it was bouncing up and down. When I heard moans and grunting coming from it confirmed what was happening inside.

As I passed it, I saw that a guy was naked except for his socks and a long sleeve white dress shirt with his tie twisted backward. His partner- a lady, was lying back in the passenger seat with her feet pushed up toward the car's roof. Her bra was pulled up to reveal ample breasts and she was naked except for black thigh-high stockings and cream-colored high heels.

The guy was between her legs with his pale butt jacking up and down. They were oblivious and in blind bliss. Some other time I might have sat down, smoked a cigarette, and watched their show, but not tonight. I was on a mission.

Chapter 45

Continuing on, I utilized some of the techniques and training I'd learned, and taught, as a scout sniper instructor. I went along a planned route, and tried my best to avoid street lights and the occasional vehicle. I was treading quietly, purposely and methodically, and keeping to the darkness.

I was confident I was doing well, until I reached the end of a block and was hit with the glare of headlights from a car. The lights were so bright they took away the shadows I was using to hide in. An alley was directly to my right, so I pulled my best ninja move and quickly disappeared into it. Pressing my back against someone's garage, I held my breath hoping I was not seen.

When the vehicle passed me, I grew nervous. It was a police car. The unit broke the intersection of the alley, then accelerated up the street with their spotlight sweeping back and forth. I let out the breath I was holding and ran quickly to the next alley. I made it around the corner then peeped back in the direction I'd just come from.

I took one step out onto the street to see where they were and much to my dismay, the brake lights glowed red and the tires screeched rubber. The police car was quickly reversing so I ran, barely making it to the end of the alleyway before I took a sharp right turn and hid in a real narrow archway. Dressed all in black there was no way they could see me.

Everything was quiet now except for the rumble of the car's engine and the soft voices from the cops and I could see the spot light moving back and forth. My heart was beating at a rapid pace and I was hoping they were lazy cops because it would be a real problem if they were ambitious, and decided to get out and investigate on foot.

After a few minutes, I heard one of the cops say, "I swear I fuckin' just saw a guy run down there!"

The other cop said, "Well, he ain't there now. Fuck that yo'! Let's go home, we're almost ten-seven." Then they accelerated away.

I paused to get my breathing in order and that was when I realized how terribly wrong things could have gone if those police had caught me. Being Baltimore, I was sure my capture by those Charm City constables would most likely involve a beating, or worse.

I smiled, leaning into the shadows after having eluded the patrol cops and making it to my destination. I was in a no-name narrow alley which bisected a strip of row houses that dead-ended on the street of businesses.

Just like Egbert was talking about, looks like he was in the bar. His shitty-work vehicle was parked at the mouth of the passage, barely a dozen feet away.

It was dark where I stood only illuminated with light of the rising full moon and a weak yellow bulb humming over a side door of the corner row house.

A row of seven foul-smelling trashcans lined the opposite side of the alley. This was a typical neighborhood: the curbside was mostly clean, but the backstreets were funky-dirty spaces. Someone had tossed a bag of trash with terrible aim, leaving it busted open and spilling.

I decided the cans offered the best concealment. So, after shining my penlight to find the cleanest spot, I tried to ignore the smell, and tucked myself behind them.

When I settled into a comfortable enough position, I pushed open the cans as quietly as possible. Now through a gap, I had a clear line of sight down the alley and across the street toward the front door of the bodega/bar.

Between the funk surrounding me and the potential for rats, I was wondering if this mission made sense. If Egbert came out with company that resembled strippers, I would need to adjust. Dancers carry large amounts of cash, so being potential targets, they're always armed and packing.

I crossed my fingers, sat still, mouth-breathing to minimize the stench, and hoping the rats in this block didn't know the ones around my street or have a communication network.

Chapter 46

The moon's shift let me know it was now past midnight. Ten minutes later, a laughing couple emerged from the Mt. Vernon Dew Drop Inn, climbed into a car, and vanished into the night.

It was quiet until the door creaked open at the row house across the alley from me. An old woman stood behind a screen door silhouetted in her lighted kitchen. She sported fat hair rollers under a paisley scarf, and neon-pink slippers. The back-light rendered her mauve nightgown entirely transparent. Leaving nothing to my imagination.

She stuck her head out, scanned up and down the alley, and then stepped out carrying a bag of trash. *Oh shit.*

If she spotted me, she'd either scream bloody murder or drop dead of a heart attack. I yanked my bandana up and pulled my hoodie low over my eyebrows. My heart hammered as she came across the street and shuffled past me, completely oblivious. Three cans down, she deposited her bag and went back to her kitchen.

She paused at her door, shaking her head at Egbert's van and at the bar beyond before retreating back inside. Only then did I let out my breath. I wiggled into a more comfortable spot leaving my bandana up over my nose, and waited. Closing my eyes I tried to meditate through the stench, and accidentally fell sleep.

A creak snapped me awake. I sat up annoyed with myself for having nodded off. Then the van shifted, the driver's door squeaked open on rusty hinges, and a figure crept out.

In the weak glow of the streetlight, I saw a man whose silhouette was unmistakable. His size, the gait—it was Egbert. While I was watching the bodega-bar, he'd been hunkered down in that van the entire time.

He had on the same clothes and dingy-white Chuck Taylors, but this time he also wore a ski mask. As he moved, I saw a glint of a gold chain at the collar of his shirt. He tip-toed away from the van and vanished from my line of sight. It looked like he was on a mission of his own.

I was sure he was up to no good, so I decided to wait and see what his deal was. Minutes later, he slithered back into view. In one hand, he clutched a Tiffany-style table lamp, its power cord trailing behind him on the asphalt. Tucked under his other arm was a VCR with AV cables wrapped around it.

He eased the van's side door open with practiced movements and gingerly set the loot inside. I leaned out for a better look, and was stunned by what I saw in the van. Besides a few handyman tools the van held other items. He wasn't just a jewelry thief-Egbert was gutting houses.

In the van, I spotted a nineteen-inch TV, a Betamax player, and a chandelier with every bulb intact. There was a four-piece stereo, a milk crate of albums, and a rolled-up Persian rug in maroon and gold.

A Dole banana box, cameras and rolls of Kodak film spilled out. He'd even raided someone's kitchen of a microwave, a crockpot, blender, and a pressure cooker. I ducked back down just as he slid the door shut and vanished across the street.

I wasn't interested in the loot; I was only concerned about one thing, and I was already developing a plan. I waited a beat, then snuck my way down to the street.

On the left corner, was a boarded-up house that had concrete steps leading down to a basement unit. Egbert would have to pass by there on his return trip to his van.

I swept my penlight into the below street space to make sure it was empty. It was, but the heavy stench of piss and mildew confirmed that this was the neighborhood urinal. I went down and folded myself into a corner and waited.

Chapter 47

I heard him returning and tried my best to only take short breaths as I waited, looking up to the sidewalk from my hiding spot. When Egbert finally appeared, he strained to balance a computer monitor stacked on top of a dot matrix printer. He stopped at the side of the van, wrestling with the electronics, trying to slide the door open. As he continued his clumsiness, I tiptoed up the steps towards him.

Once I made it up to the sidewalk, I must have made a sound because Egbert suddenly looked over his shoulder in my direction. I rewarded this action by slapping his mask-covered head with the blackjack I was carrying. It whistled as I swung it, as if I was cranking a bat to hit a homerun. It landed along his jawline with a hard whap.

When it made contact, I was sure I had killed him, but then he softly said, "Oh, momma" as his knees collapsed beneath him and he started to slide down the side of the van. With one hand still on the sliding door, he tried to stop his fall by grabbing the handle, but it didn't help.

He was yanked sideways as the door slid open with a--*sshhhh*--dragging him along. When it came to a full stop with a loud *clunk,* the office equipment he was carrying flew from his arms.

The printer went to the left and made a loud scraping sound as it clattered to the sidewalk; pieces of plastic and metal bounced everywhere. The monitor flipped into the night air to the right. The screen exploded and showered the sidewalk with glass, breaking the silence of the night. I stood there watching as it continued to flip down the sidewalk like a scene from a movie in slow motion.

With the sudden noise, lights starting going on in a few apartments. A window above the bail bond office opened and a guy leaned out trying to get a view of what was happening on the other side of the van. He shouted "Egbert, you okay over there?"

His loud voice startled me but I reacted like I'd been taught: *Move fast, get in, and get out*. I squatted and rolled Egbert. His chest was going up and down, so I was happy he was still alive, even though his jaw sat at a crooked angle. A long dribble of pink slobber ran out of his mouth beneath the mask, and a small trickle of blood seeped from his ear.

When I spied the gold chain at the nape of his neck, I reached down and snatched it, but it held firm. All I managed was to yank his head up, only for it to bang right back down on the red cobblestones. Ouch!

It took me a few seconds to locate the clasp on the necklace, and I suddenly smelled something like ammonia. I looked around for the source of the smell and saw the dark stain blooming from the front of Egbert's jeans, spreading up past his belt. He had pissed himself.

I finally worked the clasp loose, balled the necklace into my fist and shoved it into my pocket. There was a bundle of money sticking out the breast pocket of his flannel shirt, so I relieved him of that too.

A window above me opened and the old lady from earlier stuck her head out. She looked down at me standing over Egbert's prone body, and screamed for all she was worth. By the time she had gathered enough breath for another scream, I was already running.

I made it through the alley and around the corner. My adrenaline surged as sweat poured from my body. Three blocks away, after weaving through so many alleys, I had lost my sense of direction. I slowed to a walk and tried to get my breathing under control. It was time to change.

I found a dark enough corner, took off my hoodie and quickly pulled the sleeves inside out. I flipped it around, and like magic, it was white. I tied it around my waist. Unknotting the bandanna from around my neck, I wiped the sweat from my face and tied it on my head in a cook's style.

I shoved the sap down into my underwear, horizontal across the bottom of my butt cheeks, and tucked the necklace and wad of cash in the front, under my testicles.

I unclipped the Ka-Bar from my belt and shoved it down into my right boot. The least illegal thing I had on my person was the penlight, so I left it in my left back pocket. I rolled the sleeves of my T-shirt up to my shoulders.

I emerged from the darkness, lit a cigarette, and continue my walk at a casual stroll. I could hear the police radio transmissions and accelerating engines echo off the row houses. I caught flashes of their strobing lights as I kept walking with my heart pounding.

When I had put at least six blocks between myself and them, I started to relax. I hoped they stayed where they were, and didn't spread out the hunt to this area. I knew if they came upon me "Walking While Black" in the wee hours of the morning, I was sure to be stopped.

After a few more turns, I was relieved to see that I was only two short blocks from my patio-garden gate, and home.

As I was about to turn into my alley I froze when I saw the headlights of a car coming towards me. Just as I was about to bolt, I was relieved to see it was just a civilian car. I briskly walked to my entrance and got in as fast as I could. I turned the locks, leaned against it and sighed. I'd had made it home.

I started to grin from ear to ear with the thought that once they saw inside Egbert's van, their efforts would undoubtedly shift—from searching for the assailant of 'Egbert the Victim' to the investigation of 'Egbert the Burglar'. That block was probably teeming with curious residents awakened by the ruckus only to discover their neighborhood handyman, and good-time drunkard, had been robbing them blind.

Chapter 48

When I quietly opened my apartment door, in what was becoming his routine, Lucky was waiting for me. He allowed me to scratch his head before he went past me to do whatever he needed to do. It was now 2:35 a.m.

I quickly put away the sap, Ka-Bar and penlight then used some dish detergent to wash and rinse the necklace.

As I looked at the necklace, I could see why it made Egbert's mouth water and his hands itch to steal it. The medal was the size of a US dollar coin. It was a heavy circle of silver, bordered by a raised laurel of gold, and overlaid on a red star with the profile of a helmeted centurion in its center that hung on a thick gold rope. I rummaged in my sock drawer, found a white ankle sock whose partner had become MIA, and slipped the necklace inside. I opened the freezer and tucked Liz's salvaged legacy under a partial bag of chicken wings.

After a few minutes, Lucky come back inside so I locked the doors and stripped down right there in the living room. I put the sweaty clothes in a trash bag and stuffed it at the bottom of my dirty clothes hamper. I then had a long steamy shower, washing and rinsing several times until I felt clean.

Back at the breakfast bar, I realized my hands were shaking. The adrenaline was still humming through my veins as I counted the cash I'd "emancipated" from Egbert.

My haul totaled $587. Sixty-eight of which was in two-dollar bills—thirty-four of them. I meticulously tore the corners off every single deuce to bleed out the bad luck. No wonder I'd caught Egbert slipping. He clearly didn't know the superstition. I tucked the cash inside a copy of Darwin's *The Descent of Man,* then lit a cigarette. I followed the first drag with a heavy shot of Old Crow and Löwenbräu chaser.

As I smoked and sipped, a brief pang of guilt surfaced as I thought about what condition Egbert was in. He was likely horizontal in the ER by now, drifting toward a future of wired jaws and a bedside visit from the burglary detectives.

My remorse didn't last long. I drowned it out in another round of drinks and a couple of hits from a spliff. Calmed, buzzed, and proud of myself, I crawled into bed and let sleep pull me under.

I was jolted awake at 8:07 a.m. by a sound so jarring my first instinct was to reach for my gun. It sounded like a break-in, but that seemed too bold for a Tuesday morning. I sat up, held my breath, and realized the noise was coming from inside.

I crept to the edge of the bed, I peered out the door and found the culprit. Lucky was on his hind legs, stretched to his full, tiny height, mid-assault on his scratching post. I watched him work, his claws gouging and etching the catnip-scented hemp rope with a rhythmic violence. I was glad he'd finally taken to it, but I hoped this wasn't my new alarm clock.

Unable to fall back asleep, I started a pot of coffee and did some stretching exercises. I was a little sore from the night's adventure. Lucky meowed to get my attention and bolted for the door, demanding to be let out. I obliged, then stood there sipping my brew while Oprah Winfrey anchored the morning news. When I heard movement upstairs, I grabbed the frozen sock from the freezer and headed up there.

At the top of the steps I could hear Katie in the kitchen singing along to Radiohead's song *Creep.* I knocked on the door and she shouted, "Come on in."

Katie was standing at the kitchen sink drying dishes. The only clothes she had on was a purple tank top and matching panties that did nothing to contain her ample ass cheeks.

She looked at me over her shoulder and said, "Morning, AJ."

She wasn't shy or embarrassed, because she never stopped what she was doing. "I just brewed a pot. You need a cup of coffee?"

Trying not to stare at her ass, I said, "No thanks. I've had a cup. Do you know if Liz is up and moving around yet?"

"I'm pretty sure I heard both those bitches walking around up there. I'm going up now, so I'll let her know you're down here. See you later, AJ."

Katie was a thick-bodied, attractive young woman full of self-confidence. It was apparent in the way she sashayed and swished her way up the stairs, knowing full well I was watching her ass.

Chapter 49

Liz came down the stairs a minute later in a cinched robe, scowling with a bad case of bedhead. Shuffling through their common area into the kitchen, she gave me a weak smile, a hand wave, and went straight to the coffee pot.

As she poured herself a cup, I said, "Good morning. How ya doing?"

She grunted a greeting and slumped into a dining chair. After a heavy slurp of coffee, she sighed. " I'm not looking forward to today. I'm telling my father about the necklace this morning. Better to get the drama over with before class than keep dodging his calls. I can already hear the lecture."

I stayed quiet, which made her look up. "Why you so quiet, AJ?"

I reached into my pocket and gave her the ankle-sock. She knew what it was instantly. Turning the mini-sock the necklace spilled out into her palm.

The look that came across her face was a mix of relief and elation. She held the necklace to her heart and cried. She snorted snot and then screamed, "Fuck yeah!" She jumped toward me and wrapped me in a body-slamming hug. On her tiptoes, she kissed me on my cheek. "Thank you, AJ! Thank you so much."

Her forehead creased and she pushed me away. "That fucker Egbert had it, didn't he? How did you get it back?"

"Yeah, he had it but I'd rather not say how I got it back."

Her eyes narrowed. "Maybe I should still report him to the police!"

"Naw, believe me Liz. It's better to not involve the police. You won't have to worry about him ever again. Just call your dad and tell him that Egbert makes you all feel uncomfortable. Tell him what he does and that you all don't want him to ever come back here again."

Still clutching the necklace to her heart, Liz glanced at the digital clock on the stove. "Oh damn! I gotta get going." She gave me another hug and a big smooch on my chin. "Thank you, thank you again, AJ. You just saved our lives. We're gonna have to party to celebrate."

She ran up the flights of stairs. Upstairs somewhere, I heard her scream, "We ain't gotta move, bitches!"

I grinned, shaking my head as I headed back downstairs. Lucky was waiting by the door, looking personally offended that I'd left him alone. I scooped him up and set him on the breakfast bar, distracting him with a fishy, cheesy treat so I could tend to his bad eye. He grumbled his disappointment between chews, but he didn't fight.

Afterward, I took him out to the patio. To my surprise, he stayed settled in my lap, content to watch the world go by. We sat there in the morning air—me with my smoke and another fresh cup of Joe, him with his pride—as I scratched him behind his floppy ear.

Lucky and I heard the house front door slam shut three different times within a few minutes, which signaled the ladies' departure. My pager chimed and I thought about getting up to see who was hailing me, but the world seemed too right at the moment to move and possibly create a negative wobble, so I didn't get up. If it was something really important, they'd leave a message with my service.

After a while, we both snoozed right where we sat, until the sound of a sanitation truck came up the alley. Inside, I sat Lucky on his favorite perch, the top of the sofa back, and checked my pager. I had a message from the GM at my new job, informing me that training would begin Monday morning at 8 a.m.

I recalled, that Micah, the Concierge at The Regency Hotel, recommending the Towson Town Center Mall to guests. I needed to get rid of any possible negative karma-so I decided to go on a shopping spree and spend every penny of the, ill-gotten money I'd *liberated* from Egbert.

Chapter 50

After buying Dickie's workpants, CD's, a dozen pack of underwear, graphic novels and writing supplies, I ended my shopping spree on the top floor at Jenny's Bloom Garden. I'd seen on the directory that they had a skylight and it didn't disappoint—it flooded the store with a wash of natural light that made the store feel like a high-class conservatory.

A bubbly sales associate with blonde dreadlocks gave me the grand tour. When I mentioned my dull patio and my new kitten, she steered me toward oxygen-rich plants that wouldn't poison Lucky if he decided to take a nibble.

Before I knew it, we were loading up a cart. She had such an infectious personality that it didn't take much for her to cajole me into multiple purchases. She guided me to buy a parlor palm, an aloe vera plant, a star jasmine bush, and a cast-iron plant; along with a bag of potting soil and four ceramic pots. Luckily, they offered a money-back guarantee on the plants, in case my thumb turned out to be less than green.

I rounded out my haul with a medium sized hand trowel, new patio chair cushions, twenty-five feet of programmable string-lights and a set of solar motion detection lights, a wind chime with a gong sound, and finally a "Welcome Home" mat. Next door at Dr.'s Pet Shoppe, I found a studded leather collar for Lucky to match his attitude.

It was clear that it wouldn't be the smartest move for me to take the bus home with all the bags I had so instead of tempting fate, I called Driver.

As I placed my bags into the car, Driver gave a low whistle. "Well, bro—looks like you've been in there treating yourself right."

We had a nice ride back into the city as I caught him up on my new gig. When we reached my place, we dapped up and I handed him a fifty.

"That's your fare plus a tip," I said. "If this job pans out like I think it will, I'll be needing a regular lift instead of riding that late-night bus."

He grinned, pocketed the cash, and rolled out.

I left the plants, soil, and lights outside on the patio. I'd deal with those tomorrow. Inside, I stashed the rest of my haul, then collapsed onto the couch next to Lucky for a much needed nap.

Chapter 51

The next morning I had to do laundry so I humped my duffle over to the laundry mat and found the two older ladies back at their posts, but the teasing was gone. We settled into an easy rhythm of small talk, and I asked how long they'd been in the neighborhood.

Their stories painted a picture of a lost era—a place where families actually took root. Then came the "white flight," followed by a slow-motion rot. They'd watched properties crumble and dope flood the streets, bringing the crime rate with it. They described a world where businesses shuttered, services dried up, and the police shifted from neighbors to an occupying force. According to them, it was the same scenario across the city for working class people, no matter their color.

When my laundry was done, I headed back across the street. It was hard to miss the black Mercedes 560 with dark-tinted windows that sat idling at the edge of the park, right where the alley met the end cap of Bolton Street. My guard was up.

As I reached my gate, the car rolled down the alley and pulled up directly behind me. My instincts went from idle to high alert. Instinctively I reached for one of the knives I normally carry but was angry with myself when I realized that today of all days, nothing was not there. My heart was racing.

Then the driver's door swung open and a massive white guy in a black suit and tie stepped out. He was looking like some sort of government agent.

"Excuse me," he said, his voice flat but friendly. "Are you Alicide Jefferson Porter?"

"Yes," I replied, squaring my shoulders. "What can I do for you?"

At this point I really didn't know what to expect, but I was prepared to fight.

He reached into his jacket and withdrew a thick envelope. "This is for you."

My shoulders relaxed and with hesitation I took the envelope. Then he offered a polite smile and wished me a nice day.

As he backed the Mercedes down the alley, the sun caught the diplomatic plates. I looked at the envelope in my hand and then stuffed it in my laundry bag.

Inside, Lucky and I did our usual passing of the guard in the hallway but I was distracted. I was anxious to know what was in the envelope.

I sat on the couch and tore into it, only to find a handwritten note in deep black ink. The paper was heavy, expensive, and embossed with a lavender-tinted Spanish coat of arms. I began to read.

Not quite believing what I was seeing, I re-read the letter, and the attached contract, two more times. All three times it read the same:
"Mr. Porter, please accept my sincere gratitude for the return of my daughter's necklace. It is an invaluable piece of our family history, and I deeply appreciate your efforts to retrieve it.

Elizabeth has shared with my wife and I that she and her friends feel safe with you in the house. Hearing that you are a good man, and a friend to them, gives us an immense sense of peace as parents.

As a token of my appreciation, please find the enclosed rental contract with a modified monthly lease.

As you can see, I have waived all current and past fees for your pet. However, should you relocate, you will remain responsible for any potential damages. Please review, sign, and return it in the provided envelope at your convenience.

To that end, I wanted to let you know that I have hired a new management agency to handle all future maintenance at the house. The previous contractor has been terminated and will not be returning to the property.

Lastly, if I can ever be of service to you in a personal or professional capacity, please do not hesitate to call upon me."

Fernando Ortiz Castellana,

Assistant Minister of the Interior—Spain

I took a deep breath to calm myself. Now my heart was racing for a good reason. Only days ago, I'd sat in this exact spot, paralyzed by PTSD-driven panic about a grim future. Now I had not only a new job, but also a new lease that slashed my rent to less than half of what it is currently.

When Lucky hopped onto the back of the couch, I held the note up to his good eye, and with a huge smile I said, "Can you believe this, kid? KARMA!!!"

<u>**Chapter 52**</u>

With a new and improved outlook on life, I decided to keep myself busy. So, I rolled a joint, and after a couple pulls; with a new blast of herbal motivation, I went to work out in the patio-garden.

I repotted the plants into the new pots, placed them in planter boxes and scattered gray pebbles around each one. After a break with a cold beer and a little more *medicine*, I positioned and angled the motion lights. I strung the Xmas lights with adhesive strips that surprisingly held along the concrete walls.

Hearing the girls gathered in the kitchen, I went up and knocked on their door.

"'C'mon in, AJ!" they called out in unison.

I pushed the door open, but did not go in. I just invited them to come see the new garden when they had a minute. They promised to come down in a few.

As they came down the steps to the patio, I couldn't help but smile. It felt good to be part of their group—like I was their big brother and protector.

They loved the new additions, offering plenty of *oohs* and *aahs*. I felt myself blush and eventually led them inside for a short tour of my place. It was the first time they'd seen it.

I broke out icy cold blackberry brandy and a fat joint. Before long, we were settled outside in a circle, sipping drinks and passing around smoke. When the joint reached Katie, she took a long pull and exhaled through her nose. She coughed clearing her throat, cocked her head and looked at me through slitted eyes.

"Funny coincidence, isn't it? You get Liz's necklace back yesterday, and today I saw on the morning news, that some local handyman turned out to be a serial burglar, hitting the very businesses and homes he worked in."

She passed the joint to me, her gaze never wavering.

"Apparently, someone caught him in the act—and really worked him over before the cops arrived. He's in the ER now under police guard but they haven't released his name yet."

The patio went still and she continued, "I'm going to bet that guy is Egbert...and it's you who fucked him up."

I smiled a little. "I'm not admitting to anything. But, if I had done it, I would have only been doing what I thought was right thing."

They peppered me with more questions—but eventually gave up when I didn't answer. Robin had the final word. She raised her cup into the center of us, grinning.

"Well, fuck Egbert! And thank you AJ, for making sure he never comes around here-again!"

We all toasted to that.

We polished off the brandy, and killed the last of the joint. I ordered a Chinese pizza-which was becoming a house favorite. I picked up more beer, and we ate and drank until it was all gone. Even Lucky got scraps of cheese and pepperoni.

Our impromptu party came to a close with Katie and Robin giving me hugs and dap. Elizabeth just shook my hand firmly, smiling at me.

After the girls headed upstairs, I cleaned the patio to the pulse of Bob Marley and the Wailers "*Natural Mystic*". As the reggae filled the air, I smiled, realizing that those three girls were more than just my housemates—they were my *Family and Friends.*

Was I finally stumbling into my real purpose? Standing in the gap for people. Being a protector. It felt right in a way I hadn't experienced since the Marine Corps. There might even be a way I could make a living out of it.

Back inside the apartment I pulled out a new composition notebook and a fresh pen, sat down, and started writing the words you've been reading.

I wrote until the morning light began to creep through the blinds. I only quit when my fingers throbbed and a dull ache settled in my palm.

I stopped realizing I couldn't get it all down in one take. Not a life and story like mine. I'd continue transcribing another day.

But believe me, there are more adventures and tales to come of---**The Accidental Detective.**

www.ingramcontent.com/pod-product-compliance
Lightning Source LLC
Chambersburg PA
CBHW071500140726
47997CB00005B/1804